BIBLICAL ETHICS

Ethics for happier living

by
Leroy Forlines

Randall House Publications
114 Bush Road P.O. Box 17306
Nashville, Tennessee 37217

BIBLICAL ETHICS
© Copyright   1973
Randall House Publications
Nashville, Tennessee
ISBN 0-89265-014-1

All of the Bible quotations in this volume are from the authorized King James Version of the Bible.

Printed in the United States of America

Dedication

This book is dedicated to those who have taken my classes on ethics. It has been their interest, questions, and response that has encouraged the development of the system of thought set forth in this book.

CONTENTS

LESSON 1

The Theological Foundation 7

LESSON 2

The Theological Foundation Continued 22

LESSON 3

Basic Values 37

LESSON 4

Basic Relationships 52

LESSON 5

The Old and New Covenant Approaches to Ethics . . . 68

LESSON 6

Basic Principles in Studying Ethical Truth 83

LESSON 7

Christian Liberty 99

LESSON 8

Principles Versus Legalism 114

LESSON 9

Realistic Idealism Versus Perfectionism 129

LESSON 10

When Values Conflict 145

LESSON 11

Personal Development and Personal Relationships . . 161

LESSON 12

The Christian and the Material World 177

LESSON 13

The Christian's Use of Leisure Time 193

1 | The Theological Foundation

Introduction
A. What Is the Bible?
B. Who Is God and What Is He Like?
  1. God Is a Personal Being
  2. God Is the Sovereign Ruler and Judge of the Universe
  3. God Is a Holy God
  4. God Is a God of Love
  5. God Is a God of Wisdom
  6. God Is a Perfect Being
C. Who Is Man and What Is He Like?
  1. Man Was Created by God
  2. Man Was Created in the Image of God
  3. Man Was Created for Four Basic Relationships
  4. The Fall of Man Affected the Image of God in Man
  5. Redemption Is Designed to Restore the Image of God in Man

7

INTRODUCTION

We may not use the word "ethics" very often, but the ideas involved in ethics constantly occupy our minds. Whenever we ask the questions, is it right? is it wrong? is it good? is it bad? we are thinking about ethics. Ethics is concerned with morals and ideals. Morals are concerned with right and wrong. Ideals are concerned with good and bad.

We cannot ignore morals and ideals. They are woven into every yard of the fabric of life. We may violate our standards, but only at a price. We may fall short of our ideals, but not without concern. It is as if we have an ethical nerve system that responds to every life situation. Anyone who wishes to be happy must take these factors into account.

In developing a system of ethical thought, the first question to ask is: What is man? It is only when we separate man from the animal kingdom that we need an ethical system. Animals are non-moral. This being true, we need to know who man is before we can talk intelligently about moral responsibility. When man is described as one who is created in the image of God (Genesis 1:26), it follows that we must know who God is before we can know who man is. This means that though we begin our questioning with what is man, we do not begin our study at that point. We must make our study of God a prior subject of study.

When we think about studying God, we are confronted with the question of authority. What is our source of information? If we have no source of authority, we are left on the sea of speculation. The need for settling the question of authority introduces our first subject of study in laying the theological foundation for the study of ethics.

A. WHAT IS THE BIBLE?

It is not our purpose to give a defense of Biblical authority, but simply to explain the Christian viewpoint. The Bible is God's message to man. If we deny this, God becomes an object of philosophical speculation. We have no objective basis for deciding whose speculation is right. It makes us one who is "ever learning, and never able to come to the knowledge of the truth" (2 Timothy 3:7).

It is this writer's conviction that God has revealed himself, His plan, and His way of life in the Bible (1 Corinthians 2:9, 10). The Bible is an inerrant and infallible source book for moral and spiritual truth. Second Timothy 3:16 reads: "All scripture is given by inspiration of God, and is profitable for doctrine, for reproof, for correction, for instruction in righteousness."

The Bible is our authoritative source for answers concerning God, man, and morals. Those who recognize the authority of the Bible can know the truth of Jesus' words when He said, "And ye shall know the truth, and the truth shall make you free" (John 8:32). We need only to look around us to know that where the Bible is being rejected as a moral and spiritual authority moral and spiritual confusion is the result.

B. WHO IS GOD AND WHAT IS HE LIKE?

God Is a Personal Being. As a personal being He is rational and moral. He thinks, feels, and acts. He communicates himself. He is one with whom we can have a personal relationship. We can have fellowship with Him. All of our responsibility to God must be understood in the context of a personal relationship with God.

God Is the Sovereign Ruler and Judge of the Universe. He is the King of kings and Lord of lords (1 Chronicles 29:11; Daniel 4:35). He is the Supreme Being. He is above all creatures. He is the Moral Lawgiver of the universe. We are responsible to Him. One day we will stand before Him and give an account of our lives (Romans 14:12; Revelation 20:12). God is ruler. We are His subjects. We must look to Him for moral truth since we are morally accountable to Him. We must not argue with God. We must listen to Him. He has spoken to us through the Bible.

God Is a Holy God. In the Bible we learn about the moral nature of God. He is both holy and loving. First, we will give attention to His holiness (Exodus 15:11; 1 Samuel 6:20; Psalm 99:9; Isaiah 5:16; 6:1-3; 1 Peter 1:15, 16). When we think of God as being holy,

10

we think of Him as being absolutely separate from sin. We think of Him as being absolutely pure. He has not the slightest taint of sin. It was this thought which caused John to say in 1 John 1:5, "God is light, and in him is no darkness at all."

Righteousness and justice are attributes that flow from God's holiness. When we think of God as being righteous, we mean that every thought, word, and deed of God is right. There is no unrighteousness in Him.

Justice is righteousness as it is manifested in God's judicial proceedings. As a God of justice, God demands that sin receive its appropriate punishment. This is called *retributive justice*. God's justice also results in the guarantee that obedience will be properly rewarded. This is called *remunerative justice*.

God as a holy God will not tolerate sin. The first recorded revelation of God's holiness is a revelation of judgment. He said to Adam and Eve, "But of the tree of the knowledge of good and evil, thou shalt not eat of it: for in the day that thou eatest thereof thou shalt surely die" (Genesis 2:17). God's judgment against sin is His determination to remain holy. To compromise with sin would be to compromise His holiness. God will not compromise His holiness.

The acts of judgment in Biblical history bear testimony of God's hatred toward sin and His determination to be holy. The flood, Sodom and Gomorrah, and the many other acts of judgment in the Scriptures leave us no doubt where God stands on the sin issue.

The eternal punishment of the wicked reveals the

11

intolerant attitude of God toward sin. The Bible speaks of the punishment of the wicked with such expressions as, "outer darkness," "furnace of fire," "everlasting fire," "everlasting punishment," "fire unquenchable," "everlasting destruction from the presence of the LORD, and from the glory of his power," and "the lake which burneth with fire and brimstone, which is the second death."

The cross of Jesus Christ also reveals God's determination to remain holy. The cross of Christ is an eternal testimony of the fact that God will not forgive sin unless it is first punished.

If we see in God a pattern of purity and righteousness but fail to see His hatred of sin, we have failed to understand the Biblical view of holiness. There is a feeling that goes with holiness. There is the conviction that righteousness is important. It is right, good, and proper. There is the feeling that sin is serious. It is horrible, terrible, and damnable.

Neither what God did in redeeming man nor what God did in forgiving our sins is to be understood as lessening God's hatred for sin and His love for holiness. We will look at this matter more thoroughly in the next chapter. God has not lessened His concern for our holiness.

God Is a God of Love. That God is a loving God is made abundantly clear in the Scriptures (John 3:16; Romans 5:5-8; 2 Corinthians 13:14; 2 Thessalonians 3:5; 1 John 4:7-11). By God's love is meant His affectionate concern. It is expressed in the Scriptures

12

through the words "love," "lovingkindness," "compassion," "mercy," and "grace." This love is expressed in God's concern for both man's temporal welfare and his eternal welfare.

The loving concern for God is evidenced in the Old Testament, particularly in the Psalms, but the revelation of God's love reaches a high point with Jesus. Jesus had compassion in action. He was moved with compassion when He saw the sick, the bereaved, and the hungry. One of the most heart-moving scenes in the Scriptures is described for us when Matthew relates the lament of Jesus over Jerusalem: "O Jerusalem, Jerusalem, thou that killest the prophets, and stonest them which are sent unto thee, how often would I have gathered thy children together, even as a hen gathereth her chickens under her wings, and ye would not!" (Matthew 23:37).

As moving as the show of compassion was in the life of Christ, the high point in the revelation of God's love did not come in the life of Christ. The highest point in the revelation of God's love came at the Cross. The Apostle Paul puts God's love in proper perspective in Romans 5:7, 8. In 5:7 he tells us, "For scarcely for a righteous man will one die." A righteous man is one who does what is right. He is a responsible man. Paul says we would hardly find anyone who would die for a man who was merely upright. The good man is the man who goes beyond what is required. He is generous. He is accommodating. He goes the extra mile. As we sometimes say, "He would give you the shirt off his own

13

back." Paul held out hope that some might die for the good man.

In 5:7, Paul had shown what could be expected of human love at its highest. Someone might dare to die for a good man. In 5:8, he shows how God's love towers high over human love at its highest. "But God commendeth his love toward us, in that, while we were yet sinners [not good, not righteous, but sinners], Christ died for us." He died for those who had sinned against Him.

The death that Jesus died for sinners was not just an ordinary death. It was a death in which He paid the penalty for man's sin. He suffered the full wrath of God for man's sin. For the sinless Son of God to pay the full penalty for our sins in order that we who had sinned might be saved was the highest possible manifestation of God's love. God's love for us is real. It is love in action. It is love at a cost.

God Is a God of Wisdom. We do not hear enough today about the wisdom of God. The Bible has a lot to say about the wisdom of God (Proverbs 3:19; Daniel 2:20, 21; Luke 2:40, 52; 11:49; Romans 11:33; 1 Corinthians 1:24; Ephesians 3:10). It took the wisdom of God to plan a way of redemption for man. In God's sovereign rule, He relies heavily upon His wisdom. By His wisdom He accomplishes His purposes in spite of the fact that man has a free will and sin is prevalent. The more we learn about the plan of God and God's doings the more we marvel at His wisdom.

God Is a Perfect Being. God and various things

14

relating to Him are said to be perfect (Deuteronomy 32:4; Psalm 19:7; Matthew 5:48). The interest here is not in moral perfection only, but in an overall perfection. Nothing is missing or in short measure in God. He is the epitomy of the high and lofty. All of this adds up to the fact that God is an ideal person. He has no room for improvement. There is nothing in God that needs changing or could be improved by change.

There are many things about God that we have not discussed. We have limited our discussion to those truths about God that form an essential part of the theological foundation for a system of Christian ethics.

C. WHO IS MAN AND WHAT IS HE LIKE?

Now that we have discussed the identity and nature of God, we can more intelligently discuss the statement: "Man is made in the image of God."

Man Was Created by God. Man originated in a creative act of God. He is not linked with the animal world. One of the greatest contributing causes to moral decay is to be found in the linking of man to the animal kingdom as is done by the advocates of evolution. The concept of moral accountability is considerably different for one who has risen from the animal kingdom and one who by a direct act of God was created in the image of God.

Evolution emphasizes change and progress. When this is applied to man's moral life, it undercuts the idea of moral absolutes. Morals are subject to constant

15

change. The morality of the Ten Commandments passes away with the process of change. It is obvious that such thinking is not compatible with Christianity.

Man Was Created in the Image of God. We are told in Genesis 1:26, 27 that man was created in the image of God. We get clues from Colossians 3:10 and Ephesians 4:24 regarding what is involved in being created in God's image.

In Colossians 3:10 we read: "And have put on the new man, which is renewed in knowledge after the image of him that created him." The image of the Creator in man is linked in this verse with knowledge. Knowledge is related to rationality. Therefore, we conclude that being created in the image of God involves the fact that man is rational.

In Ephesians 4:24 Paul wrote: "And that ye put on the new man, which after God is created in righteousness and true holiness." The word "after" carries with it the idea of "likeness." This likeness includes righteousness and true holiness. Therefore, we conclude that the image of God in man includes the fact that man is a moral creature.

The one word that sums up the idea of rationality and morality is the word "person." God is personal. Man is personal. The basic thrust of the idea of being created in the image of God is seen in the fact that man is a personal being.

A person is one who thinks, feels, and acts. We think with our minds. In the mind we grasp ideas. We reason. We make judgments. We draw conclusions. We size up situations.

We feel with our hearts. The heart is the seat of our emotions. With the heart we feel the reality of things. With the mind we learn from the Bible that God is holy and loving. We are able to explain to some extent what that means. With the heart it is real to us that God is holy and loving. Feeling the reality of His holiness convicts us of sin and makes us want to be holy. With the heart it becomes real to us that God loves us. It is not just a statement about God that we can repeat. When we feel in our hearts that God loves us, it becomes a source of comfort and blessing.

The heart also registers the value we place on things. We feel that it is important that we be the right kind of person and that we serve God. We feel that sin is dangerous, leads to ruin, and must be avoided. We are moved by the truth that we have grasped with our minds only when we feel the reality and the importance or value of that truth.

With the will we decide to act. We commit ourselves. We can temporarily perform actions that do not truly represent our minds and hearts. Such action can only be temporary. We can permanently commit ourselves to the truth when what the mind has grasped becomes real in the heart. Only prepared minds and hearts are capable of permanent commitments.

Sometimes the word "personality" means the same thing as person. There is usually a difference. When a difference is intended, person refers to one who has the capability of thinking, feeling, and acting. Personality

17

refers to the way one thinks, feels, and acts. A person is one who is capable of behavior. Personality refers to the way one behaves.

When Adam and Eve were created, the image of God in them included not only the fact that they were personal, but it embraced their personalities. Their thinking, feeling, and acting were compatible to the thinking, feeling, and acting of God.

Man Was Created for Four Basic Relationships. From the very start, man was designed for four basic relationships. (1) He was designed for a relationship with God. He was given a responsibility by God. He was to exercise dominion over the earth and its inhabitants (Genesis 1:26). He was morally accountable to God (Genesis 2:17).

(2) He was designed for social relationships. In Genesis 2:18, God said, "It is not good that the man should be alone; I will make him an help meet for him." While the direct reference here is to making a wife for Adam, in view of the fact that man is a member of a race, it is obvious that social relationships are a part of the design of God.

(3) He was designed for a relationship to the created order (Genesis 1:26, 28-30; Psalm 8:6-8). Man was designed for the responsibility of using the earth, plants, and animals to serve his purpose. Work was a part of the original plan of God for man. It did not involve the undesirable aspects that it does now, but work has always been in the divine plan for man.

(4) He was designed for a relationship with himself.

18

Anytime there is responsibility, there is also a place for self-examination. How did I do? How can I face the challenge that is before me?

Man was not created a blank. He was not created and placed in a vacuum. He was created for these four basic relationships. He could face the challenge of these relationships and be happy or he could fail to and suffer the consequences. This is what is involved in the freedom of the will.

The Fall of Man Affected the Image of God in Man. Man was made for righteousness and obedience to God. This was the only way he could be happy. He lived this way for a time, but sin entered the picture (Genesis 3:1-6).

Sin introduced a foreign element into man's being. Man was not made for sinning. Man and sin can never fit together in full harmony. Man needs a right relationship with God. The presence of sin puts man in a state of moral conflict and confusion.

The presence of sin causes the question to rise: Is fallen man still in the image of God? The answer to that question is yes, but not fully. The above mentioned distinctions made between person and personality help at this point. Man is still a person. He thinks, feels, and acts. To that extent, he is still in the image of God.

The greatest effect of the fall is seen in man's personality. He no longer thinks, feels, and acts in a way that is compatible with God's way of thinking, feeling, and acting. The image of God is not reflected in the personality of fallen man.

Man has a moral and spiritual constitution. This fact is not obliterated by the fall. This puts the sinner in a terrible predicament. He exists in conflict and contradiction. There are certain inescapable questions that arise in his mind on the one hand. Yet, on the other hand, the bias of sin tends to make wrong answers to these questions attractive. The problem is: Man cannot live with these wrong answers.

Man cannot escape asking such questions as: Is there a God? If so, what is He like? Is there life after death? How can I know? If there is life after death, what is it like? How do I get ready for it? What is right? What is wrong? How can I know what is right and wrong?

Our interest in this study is with the inescapable questions regarding right and wrong. Even in his fallen state, man is intensely interested in the subject of right and wrong. This is not to say that he wants to do right as it is described in the Bible. He would like to change the labels on things so he could view what he wants to do as "right." He would like for the label "wrong" to be placed on things outside his desires and on things he dislikes. It is quite obvious that it is considered by all to be a plus factor to label actions as right. It is equally obvious that to label matters as wrong is a minus factor.

The interest in right and wrong is so intense in man that the sinner cannot cope with it by a simple matter of changing labels to suit his actions. Calling a wrong action right may give an occasional relief to a person. But no man can play the game with full success. Man needs a correct knowledge of right and wrong. He needs forgiveness for his sins. He needs his life changed and brought into conformity with right.

Redemption Is Designed to Restore the Image of God in Man. Colossians 3:10, Ephesians 4:24, and Romans 8:29 make it clear that redemption is designed to restore the image of God in man. The fall affected the personality of man negatively. Redemption affects the personality of man positively. It is designed to bring man into conformity to the likeness of God in the way he thinks, feels, and acts. This is a process that is going on now and will be completed in believers in the life to come.

The unbeliever is intensely interested in right and wrong, but this very interest spells trouble for him. He is in conflict and contradiction within himself. The believer has found forgiveness of sin and is experiencing the transforming grace of God. He can afford to look at the matter of right and wrong squarely. He has grace to help him bring his life into conformity with that which is right.

The Christian is interested in the subject of right and wrong because God directs him to have such an interest. He has another reason—His own being, by the design of creation and redemption, is interested in righteousness.

2 | The Theological Foundation Continued

Introduction
A. What Is Sin?
  1. The Definition of Sin
  2. The Origin of Sin
  3. The Manner of Expression of Sin
  4. The Seriousness of Sin
B. What Is Redemption?
  1. The Nature of Atonement
  2. The Nature of Salvation

INTRODUCTION

In the previous chapter we committed ourselves to the authority of the Bible in this book. We then answered two basic questions that are essential in laying a theological foundation for the study of Biblical or Christian ethics: (1) Who is God and what is He like? (2) Who is man and what is he like? In completing the laying of the theological foundation, there are two more questions to be answered: (1) What is sin? (2) What is redemption?

A. WHAT IS SIN?

In laying the theological foundation of ethics, we need to go beyond a simple statement concerning sin. We need to take a comprehensive look at the basic nature of sin. In doing this, we must look at sin from different angles.

The Definition of Sin. Sin is defined in two different ways. One approach defines sin as a wilful transgression of a known law of God or the known will of God. The other approach defines sin as any failure to obey the known will of God and any failure to conform to the holy nature of God whether known or unknown.

It is immediately obvious that the difference between these two definitions is a matter of whether one can sin without being conscious of sinning. The first definition cited above precludes the possibility of sinning without being conscious of it. The second definition admits the possibility of one's sinning without knowing at the time that what he is doing is sin.

It is very important that we adopt the right definition. If one cannot sin without being conscious of it, this means that anything one thinks to be right is all right. To say the least, this would dampen one's interest in a diligent study of ethics. If whatever one thinks to be right is right, careless thinking seems to be rewarded.

On the other hand, if one could sin without knowing it, the door is opened for wrong convictions to cause one to sin. If sin is a serious matter, it becomes important for one to have a correct knowledge of right and wrong. A serious study of ethics is important.

In settling the question of which definition is right, we need to ask if the Bible offers any help. In Leviticus 5:17 we read: "And if a soul sin, and commit any of these things which are forbidden to be done by the commandments of the LORD; though he wist it not, yet is he guilty, and shall bear his iniquity." Verse 18 prescribed a trespass offering for the person who "erred, and wist it not." Verse 19 reads: "It is a trespass offering: he hath certainly trespassed against the LORD."

It is obvious that the reference here is to a situation that does not exist in the New Testament. However, the principle of being guilty of something that was done without knowledge that it was wrong is established. One cannot confess sins of this kind until it is known that it is a sin, but at that time it should be confessed as sin.

There may be some things where knowledge may be necessary before one could be charged with sin. For example, a person could not be charged with disobeying God's call if he had no awareness of a call. However, when it comes to moral matters, the case is different. When it comes to morality, some things are inherently right. Other things are inherently wrong. This rightness

24

or wrongness is built into the very nature of things. Under no circumstances could some things be considered right. This would apply to such matters as covetousness, adultery, envy, jealousy, murder, etc. Ignorance could never make such experiences holy. They are sin and must be viewed as such, not sin only if they are recognized to be sin.

It is our conclusion that God looks at anything that is incompatible with His holy nature as sin. We must do the same.

The Origin of Sin. The concern with the origin of sin in this study is not with the origin of sin in the universe, nor the origin of sin in the human race. Rather it is the explanation of what gives origin to sin each time sin occurs. It is interesting to note, however, that the same basic principles that are involved in giving birth to sin each time it occurs were also involved in the entrance of sin into the human race.

The first principle that is involved in giving birth to sin is *unbelief.* The serpent used this tactic with Eve in the Garden of Eden. With regard to eating the forbidden fruit, he said, "Ye shall not surely die" (Genesis 3:5). This was designed to produce unbelief in Eve. As long as she believed that to eat of the tree was wrong and would bring forth death, she would not eat of the tree. Unbelief was a necessary key to unlocking the door to sin.

It still holds true that unbelief paves the way for sin. It is doubtful that anybody looks sin squarely in the face, recognizes it to be sin and worthy of death, and then proceeds to commit sin. If such ever happens, it speaks of a very serious situation.

As a rule, before a person sins he first tries to convince himself that it is not a sin. If this should fail, he tries to diminish its seriousness. He decides it is not so bad. He thinks of something somebody else is doing that is worse. He thinks of someone, whom he thinks has a good reputation, who is doing the same thing. There is always some attempt to justify an action before we do it. To justify a sinful act is to have an unbelieving attitude toward its sinfulness. To think of sin as not being so bad is to have unbelief with reference to its seriousness.

Another principle involved in sin is *selfishness* or *self-centeredness*. The words of Genesis 3:6 describes a scene where Eve had ceased to be a God-centered person and become a self-centered person. "And when the woman saw that the tree was good for food, and that it was pleasant to the eyes, and a tree to be desired to make one wise, she took of the fruit thereof, and did eat." Allegiance to God had been sacrificed for self-interest.

Sin never makes sense until God is removed from the center of the life. Even self-interests are not served by sin if God is kept in the right place. If Eve had continued to put God first, she would have never viewed the tree as "good for food, and that it was pleasant to the eyes, and a tree to be desired to make one wise." It is only when we put our selfish interest above God's interests that we can think of sin as being desirable.

A third principle involved in the origin of sin is *immediacy*. Immediacy is interested in the now. The long range, the permanent, and the eternal are sacrificed on the altar of the immediate.

When immediacy is allowed to rule, a person will trade lasting peace and satisfaction for the pleasures of sin for a season. Alcohol may offer immediate relief to a depressed person, but the after-effects lead to more severe depression and then to more alcohol until a life is destroyed. A trip on drugs follows the same procedure. A lie delivers one from temporary trouble only to destroy one's self-respect.

Sin cannot enslave us without the principle of immediacy. Anyone can tell that righteousness pays in the long run. The person who is committed to the long-range and the eternal will be able to withstand the pressures of sin. The one who is guided by immediacy is an easy target for sin.

The Manner of Expression of Sin. The number of sins would be too numerous to catalog. However, sin expresses itself in three basic ways. These three ways are set forth in Romans 1:18. God's wrath is said to be "against all ungodliness and unrighteousness of men, who hold the truth in unrighteousness."

The Greek word which is translated "ungodliness" means lack of reverence. It may refer to active irreverence or it may simply refer to the absence of reverence. Godliness refers to reverential living. It refers to that kind of living in which God is recognized as King of kings, Lord of lords, and the Holy Judge before

27

whom all men must appear and give account of themselves. Ungodliness would refer to that kind of living that fails to properly recognize God and submit to Him. Ungodliness is manifested in the active irreverence of those who blaspheme and use the name of God in vain. It is also manifested by those to whom we refer as "good moral people." They refuse to submit their lives to God by recognizing Jesus Christ as Lord and Savior.

Unrighteousness is the failure to do right. Right is that which conforms to God's moral law. Righteousness is the conformity to God's moral standard. Unrighteousness is the failure to conform to God's moral standard.

Ungodliness is the failure to be in the right relationship with God as the person who is in every way exalted above all creation. Unrighteousness is the failure to measure up to God's moral law.

In Romans 1:18 the words which are translated "hold the truth in unrighteousness" are understood by most commentators to mean "to suppress or hinder the truth in unrighteousness." Sin expresses itself in opposition to the truth. Within the individual, sin attempts to suppress the truth that he knows. It seeks to get him to push it down into his subconsciousness while trying to get error to rule in the conscious life. This is particularly true when it comes to moral truth. Sin is a mortal enemy, not to religion as such, but to holiness. This means that we have to fight our own tendency to distort moral truth.

This suppression of the truth also extends to opposing those who would proclaim the truth. This may take the form of trying to close the mouths of those who would proclaim truth. It may also take the form of proclaiming error to replace truth.

The Seriousness of Sin. Sin is too obvious for anyone to deny its existence. If anyone should attempt to deny its existence, he is simply trying to give it another name. That something is wrong with the human race no one denies. The problem is failing to recognize the seriousness of sin. A meaningful study of ethics can be made only by those who face up to the seriousness of sin.

The seriousness of sin is seen in the fact that sin involves guilt. Guilt involves a penalty. God's attitude toward sin is seen in His judgment upon sin. The doctrine of eternal punishment is the most sobering thought in the Bible (Daniel 12:2; Matthew 18:8; 25:41; Romans 6:23; Revelation 20:10; 21:8).

The seriousness of sin is also seen in depravity. Depravity is the power of sin that brings the person into its grip. It strives to keep man away from God and to thwart God's purpose with man. It brings confusion, conflict, misery, and distress into man's experience.

It is not enough to see sin as a mistake, or to just see it as wrong. It must be seen as against a holy God. It must be seen as rightly incurring eternal punishment. It must be seen as the cause of suffering, misery, shame, disgrace, and ruin.

B. WHAT IS REDEMPTION?

Redemption is the work of God that delivers man

29

from the wrath of God and reclaims and restores him from the destructive power of sin. Redemption involves the atoning work of Christ and the application of that work in salvation.

The Nature of Atonement. Man has two needs which had to be settled by atonement. He needs absolute righteousness. God required righteousness before the fall. He still requires it of all who would come into His presence and receive His blessings. The other need was brought on by sin. Sin placed man under a penalty. This penalty must be paid. The only hope of man lay in the provision of a substitute who could provide his need of righteousness and pay his penalty for him. Jesus Christ met that need for us.

A proper understanding of atonement is very important for a study of ethics. The matter of atonement is ethical to the core. If we remove ethical considerations, we have no need for atonement and no provision of atonement.

In atonement we see the proper relationship between God's holiness and His love. Why was atonement necessary for man's redemption? It was because the holiness of God refused to be compromised. God refused to set aside His demand for righteousness. The justice of God demanded that the penalty of sin be paid before man could be forgiven. Holiness is inflexible in its demands.

The affectionate concern of God's love is seen in the meeting of the demands of God's holiness. Jesus paid the penalty brought on by man's guilt. In Isaiah

30

53:6 the prophet tells us, "The LORD hath laid on him the iniquity of us all." First Peter 2:24 reads, "Who his own self bare our sins in his own body on the tree." In Galatians 3:13 Paul says, "Christ hath redeemed us from the curse of the law, being made a curse for us."

When Jesus went to the Cross, He took our sins upon himself. To put it plainly, when He took our sins upon Him, He took our place under the wrath of God. The main suffering of Jesus Christ did not come from the Roman soldiers. The main suffering came from the hands of God. Isaiah 53:10 reads, "Yet it pleased the LORD to bruise him; he hath put him to grief." Jesus paid the full penalty for our sins. He suffered as much on the Cross as sinners will suffer in Hell. This He was able to do because He is not only man, but He is also God.

Jesus also met our need for righteousness. He lived a perfectly righteous life. Paul speaks in Philippians 3:9 of a righteousness which is not our own, but one "which is of [from] God by faith." Second Corinthians 5:21 says: "For he hath made him to be sin for us, who knew no sin; that we might be made the righteousness of God in him."

When Jesus Christ paid the penalty for our sins and made His righteousness available to us, He made it possible "that he [God] might be just, and the justifier of him which believeth in Jesus " (Romans 3:26). God's justice was satisfied. Therefore, God can justify the one who believes in Jesus. It is important to observe that this was possible only after proper respect was paid to

God's holiness. God did not compromise His interest in holiness in saving man.

The atoning work of Christ makes it clear that holiness is the basic attribute of God. Love desired to save man, but holiness would consent only to terms on which holiness could be maintained. Love bowed to the demands of holiness and fulfilled its demands.

The Nature of Salvation. Salvation consists of justification and sanctification. Justification solves the guilt problem. The one who was under the sentence of eternal death is justified when he believes in Jesus. God demanded absolute righteousness. The believer received the righteousness of Christ. God demanded that the penalty be paid for his sins. He received the death of Jesus Christ for his penalty. He is declared in right standing with God. His sins are forgiven. He is restored to favor with God.

Justification is the gift of God. It is by faith not by works (Romans 3:28; Galatians 2:16; Ephesians 2:8, 9). Nothing could be clearer in the Scriptures than that we are justified by faith. At the same time, it is unquestionably clear that God protected all interests in holiness in providing justification. To understand justification in such a way that it weakens God's interest in holiness is to grossly misunderstand it.

Sanctification is also involved in salvation. Justification deals with the problem of guilt. Sanctification deals with the problem of depravity. Justification changes our standing before God. Sanctification changes our experience with sin and with God. In justification

32

we receive the righteousness of Christ. In sanctification we are made righteous in our own experience.

A study of the Biblical doctrine of sanctification leaves no doubt that righteousness is not optional with the Christian. Many people seem to misunderstand statements like the following: "We are saved by faith, not by works." "Salvation is by grace, which is an unmerited favor." "Salvation is a free gift." Some seem to think that God has taken a compromise or flexible position toward moral responsibility. From such a viewpoint, a righteous life on the part of a Christian would be nice, but is not a necessity.

It was addressing such a misunderstanding as this that caused Paul to raise the question: "Do we then make void the law through faith?" His answer was a quick: "God forbid: yea, we establish the law" (Romans 3:31).

The law represents moral authority and moral instructions. Paul's question was equivalent to saying: "Do we make void moral authority and moral responsibility through salvation by grace?" Paul not only negates the question, he states that salvation by grace establishes moral authority and moral responsibility.

The truth of Paul's claim that grace establishes law should be evident from our discussion up to this point. Before God would save the sinner, He required that the demands of the moral law for righteousness and a penalty for sin be met. The highest honor ever paid to the law was paid by Jesus Christ when He fulfilled the requirements of the law for a righteous life and submitted to suffering the full wrath of God for our sin. The whole work of Jesus Christ as redeemer is centered around honoring moral law.

God continues His interest in moral responsibility in the application of salvation. The only people who are ever saved are those who recognize their moral guilt and desire to have their experience with sin changed. The design of sanctification is to make God's people a holy people of whom it can be said: "That the righteousness of the law might be fulfilled in us, who walk not after the flesh, but after the Spirit" (Romans 8:4).

The design of God to make us righteous is not a design that may or may not be effective. A measure of success is guaranteed. First Corinthians 6:9, 10, Galatians 5:19-21, and Ephesians 5:3-5 make it clear that those who are characterized by gross immorality can lay no claim to salvation.

First John makes it abundantly clear that only those who are basically righteous have any right to claim to be a Christian. On the positive side, he says, "And hereby we do know that we know him, if we keep his commandments" (2:3). On the negative side, he says, "He that saith, I know him, and keepeth not his commandments, is a liar, and the truth is not in him" (2:4). In 3:10 he says, "Whosoever doeth not righteousness is not of God."

First John 3:9 is an unusually strong and clear verse on this subject. This verse refers to "whosoever is born of God." This means every Christian because every Christian is born of God. Concerning one who is born of

34

God, John says he "doth not commit sin . . . and he cannot sin." The meaning here based on the Greek tense is: "He does not go on sinning and he cannot go on sinning." It does not mean that he never sins, but it does mean that sin is not the habit of his life and it cannot be the habit of his life as long as it can be said he is born of God.

It is quite clear that John would have had no hesitancy in saying that those who do not practice righteousness are not saved (1 John 2:3, 4, 15, 16; 3:2-10; 5:4). There can be no doubt about it. The Bible says that salvation changes the life (2 Corinthians 5:17 and Ephesians 2:10). There is an interest in righteousness in the heart of a Christian.

A Christian is one who has recognized his moral guilt and unworthiness. He has come to Jesus Christ desiring to be forgiven of his sin and have his experience with sin changed. He has received a new nature through the new birth. This new nature is interested in righteousness. He has declared war on sin. He may not win every battle, but he is a soldier fighting against sin. When he sins, it is the sin of one who is defeated in battle, not the sin of one who had not declared war on sin. When he does sin there is a process that begins within him to work repentance.

The Christian is not and cannot be morally indifferent and unconcerned. There is room for moral growth, but his heart is cultivable soil. For the Christian, ethics is a subject of vital concern. Ethics is at the heart and core of Christianity. Man fell from a state of holiness into a state of sin. Redemption is designed to bring man from the state of sin to a state of holiness.

3 | Basic Values

Introduction
A. The Four Basic Values
   1. Holiness
   2. Love
   3. Wisdom
   4. Ideals
B. The Relationship Between the Four Basic Values
   1. Holiness and the Other Values
   2. Love and the Other Values
   3. Wisdom and the Other Values
   4. Ideals and the Other Values
C. The Importance of Observing the Proper Relationship Between the Four Basic Values

INTRODUCTION

In the first two chapters, we have laid the theological foundation which gives rise to and supports the Christian ethical system or structure. Basic values are the building materials from which the structure is built.

We have been using the figure of a structure built on a foundation to illustrate the relationship between the foundation and the structure in a system of thought. In a building, the foundation supports the structure, but it does not give birth to the structure. In a system of thought, the structure grows logically out of the foundation. The structure is inherent in the foundation. The structure is logically related to the foundation so that the logical consistency of the structure with the foundation becomes a test of truth for the structure. The foundation must be true for the structure to be true. If the foundation is true, and if the structure is logically related to the foundation, the structure is true.

As we approach the study of the basic values, it will be observed that these are things already evident in the theological foundation. It is important as we make this study of ethics that we see a system of thought developing.

A. THE FOUR BASIC VALUES

All morals and ideals are reducible to four basic values: holiness, love, wisdom, and ideals. A basic understanding of each of these and their relationship with each other is essential to true ethical thought and life. It will be observed that each of these values is also found in God. Holiness, love, and wisdom are attributes of God. Ideals are related to the perfection of God. He is the epitomy of the high and the lofty. As the psalmist said, "O LORD our Lord, how excellent is thy name in all the earth!" (Psalm 8:1a).

Holiness. Holiness involves separation from sin, conformity to righteousness, and dedication to God. Righteousness may be thought of as conformity to a right standard. It may be used sometimes apart from a relationship with God. Holiness always implies a relationship with God. Holiness is more than morality. There can be at least a limited morality without dedication to God. There can be no holiness without dedication to God. The person we would refer to as the "good moral person" who makes no profession of devotion to God is unholy. Holiness embraces godliness (reverential living before God) and righteousness (conformity to God's moral standard).

Sin and holiness are opposites. Holiness is separation from sin in thought, word, and deed. Man will not achieve absolute holiness in this life, but we dare not define holiness or sin in the light of what is possible or not possible. We must look at holiness in the light of God's holiness. We must view sin as that which is not compatible with God's holiness.

It is important that we not limit our look at the moral aspect of holiness to the negative aspect. There is more to health than the removal of disease. Righteousness is not just the absence of sin. Righteousness is essentially positive. To fail to stand for sin is essential to standing for righteousness, but standing for righteousness requires positive action for righteousness. We must be for honesty, purity, duty, responsibility, reliability, etc.

The whole matter of separation from sin, conformity to righteousness, and dedication to God must be real to a person before there can be Christian holiness. A superficial, shallow approach to the matter will not do. It does not produce holiness. Thoughts about sin and righteousness are not adequate if they cannot be described as conviction. Thoughts can occur in the mind with little or no heart involvement. Convictions exist only when the heart is deeply involved.

Standards are not convictions unless they are deeply rooted in the heart. Standards that are less than convictions are like a steel pipe that is driven only a few inches into the ground. Convictions are like a steel pipe that is driven deeply into the ground. They both appear to be the same until pressure is applied. The one that is driven only a few inches will topple over. The one that is deep will withstand the pressure.

Standards that are less than convictions will topple or waver when the pressure is on. Convictions are not changed by pressure. They remain firm. True Christian holiness exists only where convictions exist.

Holiness is not optional for the Christian. The writer of Hebrews tells us: "Follow peace with all men, and holiness, without which no man shall see the Lord" (Hebrews 12:14). First Peter 1:15, 16 reads: "But as he which hath called you is holy, so be ye holy in all manner of conversation; because it is written, Be ye holy; for I am holy."

Any approach to the promotion of Christianity that does not give a strong emphasis to holiness has grossly misunderstood Christianity. We should use the word "holiness" in the promotion of the concept of holiness. It is true that the concept of holiness is set forth when we talk about separation from sin, righteousness, and dedication to God. We do not need always to use the word holiness, but we need to use it frequently.

Holiness is frequently avoided because it tends to be a term of reproach. We do not need to be unnecessarily offensive. There is certainly a place for wisdom in the choice of terms. At the same time, we must preserve the Biblical vocabulary in the communication of the Christian message. One suspects that people who are embarrassed over the word *holiness* are more ashamed of holy living than they are to use the word *holiness* to describe that living. We dare not so streamline Christianity that it will lose its reproach in society. When this happens, it is time to ask: Is what we have Christianity?

Love. Love is an affectionate concern that motivates one to perform the action appropriate for the concern. These are two aspects of love—affection and action. We can frequently predict the path of action that love will take. There are some things that are incompatible with love. However, merely taking the path of action love would most likely take and merely avoiding things incompatible with love does not constitute love. Love is not reducible to a prescribed formula or code.

Love exists only when the appropriate action grows out of affectionate concern. Paul says: "And though I bestow all my goods to feed the poor, and though I give my body to be burned, and have not charity [love], it profiteth me nothing" (1 Corinthians 13:3). Both of the actions that Paul is describing are actions that one would normally attribute to love. However, Paul suggests that they can exist without love. The missing factor that robs such an action of the right to be associated with love is affectionate concern—the absence of heart involvement.

John describes a situation where the absence of appropriate action makes it obvious that love is not present. He explains: "But whoso hath this world's good, and seeth his brother have need, and shutteth up his bowels of compassion from him, how dwelleth the love of God in him?" (1 John 3:17). Love exists only when there is affectionate concern that leads to appropriate action.

Love not only leads to appropriate action toward the one loved, it also disciplines the behavior of the person who loves. Paul describes this behavior in 1 Corinthians 13:4-7.

Love leads to patience. It is not envious. It does not display itself in a boastful manner (verse 4).

Love does not behave in an unbecoming manner. It is not self-seeking. Love is not quick to be angry. It does not tend to hold the evil done to it against the people who did it (verse 5).

Love receives no pleasure from iniquity. Love receives pleasure from truth (verse 6).

Love is characterized by endurance. Love looks for the best. It does not quickly believe evil about people. Love hopes for the best (verse 7).

Love is not optional for the Christian. Jesus said the first and great commandment is our obligation to love God. The second commandment is our obligation to love our neighbor (Matthew 22:37-39).

John leaves no doubt that love for our Christian brothers must be a part of a person's experience if he is to be considered a Christian. He explains: "In this the children of God are manifest, and the children of the devil: whosoever doeth not righteousness is not of God, neither he that loveth not his brother" (1 John 3:10). He further states: "Beloved, let us love one another: for love is of God; and every one that loveth is born of God, and knoweth God. He that loveth not knoweth not God; for God is love" (1 John 4:7, 8).

According to John, a profession of faith that is not accompanied by love is of no avail. He says: "He that saith he is in the light, and hateth his brother, is in darkness even until now" (1 John 2:9).

Wisdom. Wisdom is the source of good, sound judgment. Wisdom is sanctified common sense. Wisdom weighs matters carefully in the light of eternal values. Doctrinal, moral, and spiritual truth is translated into practical truth for real life situations.

Wisdom does not live in a dream world. It does not

spend its energies conceiving idealistic answers on how to cope with the situations of life. It finds answers that are workable in a world filled with harsh reality.

Wisdom does not bow to pressures of the crowd, neither does it yield to the temptations of sin. It sees through the vain, deceitful promises of sin. Wisdom is convinced that it pays to do right. It is convinced that it pays to serve God. Wisdom was demonstrated by Moses when he "refused to be called the son of Pharaoh's daughter; choosing rather to suffer affliction with the people of God, than to enjoy the pleasures of sin for a season" (Hebrews 11:24, 25).

The Bible places a very high value on wisdom. Proverbs 3:13-18 reads:

> Happy is the man that findeth wisdom, and the man that getteth understanding.
> For the merchandise of it is better than the merchandise of silver, and the gain thereof than fine gold.
> She is more precious than rubies: and all the things thou canst desire are not to be compared unto her.
> Length of days is in her right hand; and in her left hand riches and honour.
> Her ways are ways of pleasantness, and all her paths are peace.
> She is a tree of life to them that lay hold upon her: and happy is every one that retaineth her.

See also Job 28:12-28; Proverbs 4:5-9; 8:11-21; 16:16, 20-24.

Wisdom is optional only to those who are willing to suffer the consequences. We dare not face life without it. Wisdom has never been more necessary than it is in the present world with all of its complexities.

Ideals. The concern of ideals is with excellence. Ideals embrace values such as refinement, the lofty, the beautiful, the noble, polish, dignity, poise, honor, good manners, masculinity, ruggedness, strength, femininity, charm, daintiness, and good taste. Ideals go beyond right and wrong. They speak of an area where good and bad are more appropriate judgments. For example, it may not be morally wrong to do a poor job matching colors, but it is bad taste. Or, righteousness may not be involved in drawing a beautiful picture, but it is a good work of art.

Art belongs in the category of ideals. The aim of art is excellence in a given field.

Ideals cannot be ignored by the Christian. We cannot behold the perfection of God without having an appreciation of excellence. The more we see the excellence of God, the more we desire the experience of excellence. Paul was turning our minds toward ideals when he said: "Finally, brethren, whatsoever things are true, whatsoever things are honest, whatsoever things are just, whatsoever things are pure, whatsoever things are lovely, whatsoever things are of good report; if there be any virtue, and if there be any praise, think on these things" (Philippians 4:8).

45

B. THE RELATIONSHIP BETWEEN
THE FOUR BASIC VALUES

Holiness and the Other Values. In one sense holiness embraces love, wisdom, and ideals. The fact of love is a requirement of holiness. There could be no holiness in a person who did not love. However, the precise ordering of the steps of love, except that it must not conflict with holiness, is not given by holiness.

Love must never conflict with holiness. Holiness is inflexible; love is flexible. The very nature of holiness is preserved by the fact that it is unbending. If holiness adjusted to pressure or changed to suit circumstances, it would no longer be holiness. On the other hand, the nature of love is best served by a degree of flexibility. Love that operates out of an inflexible "must" is not love. Love must express itself freely out of desire.

In view of the fact that holiness is inflexible and love permits a degree of flexibility, when there is a tension between the two, love bows to the demand of holiness. This bowing of love to holiness was clearly revealed in atonement. Holiness demanded that sin be punished; love desired to save man. Love bowed to the demands of holiness so it could fulfil its desire to save man. Man is saved on the terms required by holiness.

When no way can be found to satisfy both holiness and love, the demands of holiness will be met and love must step aside. This is exactly what will happen when sinners are cast into Hell. The greatest love in the universe will not be able to stay the hand of God's holy wrath when Christ-rejecting sinners are cast into Hell.

In our own experience we must seek to express our love, but never at the cost of compromising righteousness. We may desire to help a friend, but if lying is involved in helping him we cannot help him. We can look for other means of helping, but if righteous means cannot be found we cannot give assistance.

Holiness and love need each other. If the firm stand of holiness is not accompanied by love, it ceases to be holiness. Holiness is firm, but to be ruthless and roughshod contaminates holiness. Love needs to be accompanied by the firm hand of holiness. When this is not the case love becomes weak-kneed sentimentality. This is not love. When the desires of love are frustrated, if love is not disciplined by holiness, it runs the risk of behaving itself unseemly. This is not love.

Wisdom is also embraced by holiness. Holiness is not unconcerned when it comes to the matter of good judgment. Yet, we do not consider the full operation of wisdom to be under the controlling authority of holiness. Also, we make a distinction between poor judgment and unrighteousness.

✳ Ideals, too, are a must for holiness, but with a greater degree of freedom as to particular expression than is found with either love or wisdom. Holiness cannot ignore ideals. We may be able to distinguish between the right and the good, but when we cease to uphold the good, given enough time, we will cease to uphold the right. Good is so closely related to right that any amputation of good from right will cause right to

47

bleed and suffer loss.

In a study of ethics, it is imperative that supremacy be given to holiness. It takes the backbone out of ethics when supremacy is given to love. When anything is supreme over holiness, if any bending is done, holiness must do the bending. Righteousness must be twisted to suit the situation. Rounding corners and fudging sets in. When holiness is dethroned from the position of supremacy over the other values, it will be only a matter of time before the results become drastic and devastating.

Love and the Other Values. Love and holiness have an area of common ground. Paul says, "Love worketh no ill to his neighbor: therefore love is the fulfilling of the law" (Romans 13:10). This common ground between holiness and love embraces the morality of the Ten Commandments. However, when it comes to the matter of retributive justice love does not share a common ground with holiness. Holiness, not love, pronounces a penalty on sin and insists that it must be paid. It is a mistake to explain all of God's actions as originating in love. It is also a mistake to insist that all of our actions must proceed from love.

Some of our actions as obedient Christians are best explained as originating in love. Others are best explained as originating in righteousness and justice. Jesus' action in healing the sick is best explained as originating in love. His action of cleansing the Temple is best explained as originating out of righteousness and justice. In one sense of the word, we may think of a tension between holiness and love, but not a contradiction. Holiness and love need each other. At points of tension, love out of due respect and appreciation for holiness gives way to holiness.

Within its area of freedom, love is guided by wisdom. Wisdom is a companion to love which helps it locate its most effective path of action. It was wisdom that designed a plan of atonement whereby love could offer salvation to man and at the same time the demands of holiness could be met. Wisdom must be understood as a companion of love, not an overlord that bosses it around.

Love has a double relationship to ideals. Love itself is an ideal, but it is not reduced to a subpoint under ideals. Love should be subjected to the refining influence of ideals. In this role, ideals are a companion to love.

Wisdom and the Other Values. Wisdom can never go contrary to holiness without suffering loss. However, it is not merely a subject of holiness. It is a companion to holiness as it is to love and ideals. Wisdom seeks the proper combination of holiness, love, ideals, and wisdom. Wisdom honors the inflexibility of holiness. It is moved by the affectionate concern of love. It is challenged by the excellence of ideals. It is confident of the value of its own contribution.

Ideals and the Other Values. In one sense, ideals embrace holiness, love, and wisdom. In another sense, they embrace areas not fully touched by them. In the order of importance values such as refinement, polish, good manners, and good taste, come after holiness, love, and wisdom. In a sense these values fall under the responsibility to be holy. Holiness cannot totally disregard them. Holiness calls for a general responsibility in the area of ideals, but the degree of fulfilment, and the manner of fulfilment is left to wisdom.

Priority must be given to holiness, love, and wisdom over ideals. In a world affected by sin, these ideals cannot find complete fulfilment. Priorities often place limitations upon them. However, they are to be included in the goals of Christians insofar as they are realistically possible.

C. THE IMPORTANCE OF OBSERVING THE PROPER RELATIONSHIP BETWEEN THE FOUR BASIC VALUES

It is obvious that holiness, love, wisdom, and ideals cannot all be inflexible. If they were, the tension between them could not be resolved. Much harm is done by people when they become inflexible in a group situation where they understand love, wisdom, and ideals to be involved. Much harm is also done when they are willing to be flexible when holiness is involved.

We can respect a sincere Christian when he differs with us on a matter where holiness is involved, but we can never be a party to that which would compromise holiness as we understand it. There is a place for compromise. There is a place for negotiated settlement. For the sake of unity, we can accept a modified plan on how a group will express its love. Our own expression of love may have to recognize the flexibility of love. For example, our expression of love must be in keeping with our pocketbook. Holiness cannot condone the expression of love by a Robinhood who robs from the rich to give to the poor.

What we might consider the best judgment in a business meeting may have to be compromised by modification to keep the peace. If we regard judgment with the same inflexibility that we do holiness, division and unrest or authoritarianism is the inevitable result. We should labor for the best in judgment, but we should be able to live with less than the best.

For the most part (there are some exceptions), the matter of church music fits in the category of ideals rather than being a matter of right or wrong. When the flexibility of ideals is taken into account, it is not necessary to split a church over the kind of music we use. It is wrong to be inflexible to the point of causing trouble over what one considers the best music.

One of the most valuable lessons to be learned in life is the ability to recognize when to be inflexible and when to be flexible. When this is done we can live better with our own consciences and can fit more harmoniously into group situations.

Because of holiness, we have convictions. Because of love, we have concern. Because of wisdom, we have common sense. Because of ideals, we are challenged toward excellence.

4 | Basic Relationships

Introduction
A. The Four Basic Relationships
   1. Man's Relationship with God
   2. Man's Relationship with Others
   3. Man's Relationship with the Created Order
   4. Man's Relationship to Himself
B. The Relative Importance of the Basic Relationships

INTRODUCTION

To this point of our study, we have examined the theological foundation and the basic building supplies for a Christian system of ethics. The foundation consists of the doctrines of the Bible, God, man, sin, and redemption. The basic building supplies consist of holiness, love, wisdom, and ideals.

We now turn our attention to the basic framework of the building. This basic framework consists of four basic relationships: (1) Man's relationship with God. (2)

Man's relationship with others. (3) Man's relationship with the created order. (4) Man's relationship with himself. All of life's experiences include one or more of these relationships.

A. THE FOUR BASIC RELATIONSHIPS

Man's Relationship with God. Of the four basic relationships, our relationship with God is the primary relationship. It is our greatest responsibility. It is the relationship that gives direction to all other relationships.

Concerning our relationship with God, Jesus said, "Thou shalt love the Lord thy God with all thy heart, and with all thy soul, and with all thy mind. This is the first and great commandment" (Matthew 22:37, 38). We owe to God supreme devotion, worship, and reverence.

Our attitudes must be the same as Paul's when he said, "For to me to live is Christ" (Philippians 1:21), and "That I may know him" (Philippians 3:10). Our hearts' cry must be for a closer relationship with God. We must have a God-centered, Christ-centered outlook on life.

Our relationship with God is a personal relationship. We are persons. We recognize God as a personal God.

There is a difference in an ethical responsibility to a person and an ethical responsibility to a code or a set of laws. An ethical responsibility to a code calls for outward conformity. It easily falls into the trap of mechanical obedience because a code has no way of judging the heart. It only measures action.

In personal relationships, the interest goes much deeper than outward conformity. There is a deep interest in heart attitude. Outward conformity does not necessarily represent the proper attitude of heart. Also, there is a difference between wilful disobedience and failure to obey that comes from weakness. There is a difference in sin that comes from losing a battle, and sin where there was no battle. In personal relationships, conformity or lack of conformity is not everything. Heart attitude is important. God sees beyond the outward actions. The Word of God is a "discerner of the thoughts and intents of the heart" (Hebrews 4:12).

Occasionally, someone will say, "Christianity is a personal relationship with God, not obedience to a moral code." If properly interpreted, the statement is true. However, if it is intended to undercut the necessity of moral responsibility on the part of a Christian, it is a tragic misunderstanding of Christianity.

The fact that salvation involves a personal relationship does not mean that it cannot have essential moral results. The nature of our personal relationship with God is determined by who God is and the nature of His attributes. The devil is a person too, but no one would deny that there is a definite moral difference between a personal relationship with Jesus Christ and a personal relationship with the devil. To talk about loving Jesus and loving sin is like talking about loving the devil and loving holiness. It is a contradiction to think about loving God and not loving holiness (1 John 2:15). Love involves affectionate concern that leads to action. Affectionate concern and devotion to God leads to moral action. A personal relationship with a holy God of necessity results in moral action. While this moral action cannot be totally expressed in a code, it cannot be totally separated from the idea of a code.

It is only when our relationship to God is properly observed that we are in a position to answer questions relating to ethics. Where there is a failure or a weakness in one's love for God, moral judgment will suffer accordingly. Sound ethical judgments can be rendered only by an involved and interested person. It is only when we are deeply interested that our moral and rational abilities reach their highest peak of efficiency in matters of right and wrong, good and bad.

Man's Relationship with Others. Jesus placed a very high value on love for others. The first commandment is to love God. The second commandment is, "Thou shalt love thy neighbour as thyself" (Matthew 22:39).

Man is a "relationship" creature. Every intake of air, water, and food is a reminder of the fact that man cannot live alone. If these supplies would be suddenly cut off, a person would have a few moments of misery and then die. Man's personal needs can no more be met through isolation than his physical needs can be.

Man has social needs. A human being cannot be

defined purely in terms of an individual. He is an individual who is a member of a race. He needs others. Others need him. He must function with due regard for others. This is not simply a divine commandment. It is built into our very nature. If we isolate ourselves from others or if we are not properly related to others, our problem is more than divine displeasure. We hurt within ourselves. We are failing to supply a need that is built into our very nature. We need the fellowship.

Our first obligation to another person is to recognize him as one who is created in the image of God. This gives every human being a sense of worth. A life of sin may take away worthiness from a person, but not worth. Man is not worthy of salvation, but he is worth saving. There is always something that separates man from animals. We must hope for every man the fulfilment of the divine image in man. It is for this reason that we must be deeply concerned for the salvation of every person. It is only through redemption that God's purpose in creating man in His own image can be fulfilled.

Involved in the image of God is the fact that each person is a thinking, feeling, acting being. We should never treat people like puppets or machines. We are to influence people as thinking, feeling, acting beings, but we are never to try to control them through manipulation. We are to lead people to make intelligent decisions with their conscious minds. We are not to seek to control them by keeping them ignorant. We are to help them develop as thinking, feeling, acting beings.

We are to respect all people as made in the image of God. We are to be concerned about their needs both physical and spiritual. We are to have a special concern for those who are saved (Galatians 6:10). We must ever keep in mind the fact that we are members of one family—God's family. As partakers of a common faith and experience, we form a fellowship of saints.

We must keep in mind the fact that we are persons. Just as in our relationship with God, our moral responsibility to others is not fully expressible by a code. Heart attitude must motivate what we do for others.

Man's Relationship with the Created Order. By created order, we are here referring to the material universe and its animal inhabitants. God must be recognized as the Creator and Sovereign Ruler of the universe and its animal inhabitants, just as He is our own Creator and Sovereign Ruler. As Sovereign Ruler of both man and the created order, God has commanded men to exercise dominion over the fish of the sea, and over the fowl of the air, and over the cattle, and over all the earth, and over every creeping thing that creepeth upon the earth (Genesis 1:26).

To exercise dominion over the fish of the sea means to catch them, use them for food, and to produce the many by-products that come from fish. A similar statement can be made about the fowl of the air, the cattle, and every creeping thing that creepeth upon the earth. Included in this would be the domestication of animals to serve our various needs.

The exercise of dominion over the earth would involve mining the minerals, drilling for oil, cutting timber from the forest, etc. These raw materials would then be taken and run through the appropriate processes to make usable materials for fuel, manufacturing purposes, and for the construction of buildings, equipment, machinery, etc. One of the important aspects of exercising dominion over the earth is the cultivation of the soil to produce food, raw materials for clothing, and a number of other products.

In recent years it has become more obvious that man must be concerned about ecology in this exercise of dominion. In a heavily populated and highly industrialized area this becomes a special concern. We must care for the earth, not just use it to produce the desired products. On the other hand, we must realize that the earth, plants, and animals must be used to serve man's needs.

A proper understanding of the material universe eliminates a negative attitude toward material things. It is a misunderstanding of the Scriptures to view material things as a necessary evil to which we are to give a minimum of attention. We are not to despise material things. See Psalms 8:3, 4; 19:1; and 24:1.

A proper approach to material things comes not from depreciating them, but appreciating them. We recognize God as the giver of "every good gift and every perfect gift" (James 1:17). We thank Him. We give glory to Him. From our hearts we sing, "How Great Thou Art!" We use the material things for good, not evil, purposes. The pursuit of material things is not allowed to conflict or interfere with moral and spiritual responsibilities. Following these guidelines will help us see material things in their proper perspective.

A proper appreciation of material things also gives a sense of value to our labor with the material. The exercise of dominion over the earth and its inhabitants is a divine command. This makes the labor in fulfilling this command a divine service. Since it is a divine service, it must be done well. When seen as a divine service, housekeeping, the everyday chores of life, and the work-week take on a new sense of value.

Man's Relationship to Himself. The questions to be answered in man's relationship to himself are: (1) What opinion should a person have of himself? (2) What should a person's attitude be toward himself?

Many work on the assumption that it is wrong to have a good opinion of oneself and it is meritorious to have a low opinion of oneself. Thus, they are constantly downgrading themselves. They also feel that it is wrong for a person to love himself.

In developing one's opinion of himself, he must recognize that he is created in the image of God (Genesis 1:26). This places a high value on man. Sin makes the sinner *unworthy* of salvation. But he is *worth* saving because he is created in the image of God. Genesis 9:6 and James 3:9 provide evidence that the image of God in man gives value to man.

As Christians, when we develop our sense of self-value, we must keep in mind the fact that we have been created by God in His own image and that by redemption we are members of God's family. These facts put us on guard against careless downgrading of ourselves. We dare not downgrade the handiwork of God.

In view of the fact that the Bible condemns the sin of pride and sets forth humility as a virtue, many have felt compelled to have a low view of themselves. However, one might ask: Is downgrading oneself the way to develop Biblical humility? A feeling of worthlessness has no room for pride. There must be a sense of value before there can be pride. Humility is amazing only in people who do have a sense of value. They have a sense of value, but they recognize that without God and without the contributions made by others they would have no value. They react with humble appreciation, not with pride. They display well the discipline of love as it is set forth in 1 Corinthians 13:4, "Charity vaunteth not itself, is not puffed up."

There are some Scripture verses that have given difficulty. Romans 12:3 reads, "For I say, through the grace given unto me, to every man that is among you, not to think of himself more highly than he ought to think; but to think soberly." To warn a person not to think too highly of himself is not the same as asking a person to have a low opinion of himself. It only asks him to have an accurate opinion rather than one that is too high. Paul asked them "to think soberly." There is nothing sober about downgrading oneself. In the context Paul was saying that God has given various gifts to

Christians. These gifts are capacities for service. He was asking them not to look at themselves as capable of filling a higher place of service than that for which their gifts equipped them. They were to soberly assess their place of service in keeping with their gifts.

In 1 Corinthians 15:10 Paul said, "But by the grace of God I am what I am: . . . but I laboured more abundantly than they all: yet not I, but the grace of God which was with me." Based on the last part of the verse, many feel obligated to downgrade themselves. They take themselves to be nothing and God to be everything. Any recognition of self-value is considered pride and robbing God of His glory. Let us take the position that Paul was nothing and see what it makes the first part of the verse say. Paul would be saying, "By the grace of God I am nothing." That would not be very complimentary to God. There must be some sense of self-value before the statement has any real meaning and expresses gratitude to God. Paul was simply recognizing that had it not been for the grace of God he would have still been in Pharisaism. He would never have been an apostle. Had it not been for God's help he could not have had such a fruitful ministry. He is thanking God for making him a person of value and making his ministry fruitful. He was somebody. He had accomplished something. In that light it was an expression of dependence and gratitude that caused him to say, "By the grace of God I am what I am."

Another verse that presents a problem is Romans 12:16. Paul says, "Be not wise in your own conceits." If this is interpreted to mean that it is wrong for a person to believe that he has some degree of wisdom, it would condemn Paul's estimate of himself in 1 Corinthians 3:10 where Paul referred to himself as "a wise master-builder." It is true that Paul credited the grace of God with the fact that he was a wise masterbuilder. At the same time, the statement still indicates that Paul had a sense of self-value.

What Romans 12:16 is condemning is what we call "the big head." The person is puffed up about his own wisdom. He does not recognize his debt of gratitude to God and others. He forgets his dependent role. A person has true wisdom only as he submits to God and the authority of the Bible. Such a person will not have the big head. He will not be puffed up. At the same time he can recognize that by God's grace he has developed a degree of wisdom.

The evidence is clear that Paul had a good self-image. He had self-esteem, self-respect, and self-confidence. In 1 Corinthians 4:16 he said, "Wherefore I beseech you, be ye followers of me." Again in 11:1 he said, "Be ye followers of me, even as I also am of Christ." Paul viewed himself to be a good example of the Christian life.

Paul had self-confidence. He said, "I can do all things through Christ which strengtheneth me" (Philippians 4:13). He was not puffed up about this confidence because it was dependent upon the strength of Christ. Yet, he had confidence.

Paul's life ended with a note of self-esteem and

self-respect. He said, "I have fought a good fight, I have finished my course, I have kept the faith" (2 Timothy 4:7). There is no downgrading in this statement. There is no self-depreciation.

The Christian is simply to follow the rule of honesty in his self-evaluation. He must see his weaknesses and failures. He must also see his strong points and successes. To fail at either point is to fail to be honest. His self-evaluation must be an honest reflection upon the fact that he is made in the image of God. He is a member of the family of God. His weaknesses and failures, and his strong points and successes, must be put in proper perspective. When the facts justify it, he can have self-respect, self-confidence, and self-esteem. Such an estimate of oneself forms one of the foundation stones for happiness. Without it there can be no happiness.

Now we raise the question: Is it wrong for a person to love himself? In Matthew 22:39 Jesus said, "Thou shalt love thy neighbour as thyself." It would be a poor example to draw from in loving our neighbour if it were wrong for a person to love himself. Jesus is saying that we should have a love for our neighbor similar to the love that we have for ourselves.

Jesus' statement, "If any man will come after me, let him deny himself, and take up his cross daily, and follow me" (Luke 9:23), has caused some difficulty at this point. Some have interpreted self-denial to be much the same as self-depreciation. This is a misunderstanding of what Jesus said.

To get what Jesus said, we must read, "Let him deny himself" and "follow me" together. The self-denial is not an end within itself. It does not mean that we are to satisfy the barest minimum of our desires. We are to deny in order to follow. Where there is a conflict between our own ambitions and desires and following Jesus, we are to deny ourselves the fulfilment of these ambitions and desires and follow Jesus. The emphasis is on following Jesus, not on self-denial. Self-denial enters to whatever extent is necessary for one to follow Jesus.

To turn the emphasis on self-denial actually defeats what Jesus said. The person whose attention is taken up with self-denial is taken up with himself. He indulges in self-examination to be sure he has not missed any area of self-denial. He becomes self-centered. Whenever an unusual amount of a person's attention is taken up with himself, he is self-centered regardless of what his motive may be. Jesus was advocating a Christ-centered life, not a self-centered life.

The words of Jesus, "Whosoever will save his life shall lose it" (Luke 9:24), aptly describes the person who is taken up with self-denial. He is going to save his life through indulging in self-denial. He loves his life through over-introspection. Over-introspection produces insecurity, fear, an inferiority complex, and a loss of self-esteem. These are all enemies of happiness. His indulgence in self-denial causes him to take his eyes off Christ. Therefore, he cannot follow Christ as he should. The very purpose he sought to accomplish by indulging in self-denial is defeated.

The person who focuses on following Christ becomes Christ-centered, not self-centered. He is the one of whom Jesus speaks when He says, "But whosoever will lose his life for my sake, the same shall save it" (Luke 9:24). He does not cease to love himself, but he does set aside every ambition, plan, or desire that would conflict with following Jesus.

Some are troubled by Luke 14:26. Jesus said, "If any man come to me, and hate not his father, and mother, and wife, and children, and brethren, and sisters, yea, and his own life also, he cannot be my disciple." Let us first observe that if we take the language here with its absolute meaning it does not just refer to the attitude one would have toward himself. It refers to people that we are clearly told to honor, respect, and love. The teaching of the verse is that, if there is a conflict between following Jesus, the members of our family, or our own desires, we are to follow Jesus. The "hating" is certainly not to extend beyond these points of conflict. The teaching here is essentially the same as that found in Luke 9:23, 24.

We are to take the steps necessary in life for us to have self-esteem, self-respect, and self-confidence. We are to love ourselves. We can take care of self-interest, but we are not to become self-centered.

B. THE RELATIVE IMPORTANCE
OF THE BASIC RELATIONSHIPS

These relationships cannot be singly considered in

a person's experience. Each must be seen in the context of the other relationships. Of the four basic relationships, our relationship to God is the primary relationship. The other relationships can function properly only when this relationship is functioning properly. Our relationship with God determines the nature of the other relationships. There is a parallel here in tuning a stringed instrument. One string is tuned. The other strings are in tune only as they are in proper harmony with this string.

It is frequently said that we are to put God first, others second, and ourselves last. We put God first, but an awkward situation develops when we try to make a mathematical order out of the other two. One gets the idea that he must provide for others before he does for himself. A person cannot possibly provide for everyone else before he provides for himself.

Perhaps the best way to say it is: Self-interest must be pursued in the context of putting God first and loving others. This avoids the awkwardness. In this context, the pursuit of self-interest, self-esteem, self-respect, and self-confidence is protected from becoming self-centeredness. Taken out of the context of putting God first and loving others, the pursuit of self-interest will inevitably result in self-centeredness.

It is obvious that our relationship with the created order, while being very important, is not on par with our relationship to God, others, and ourselves. It does form an important part of life's experiences. Our relationship with God, others, and the created order are outgoing relationships. These relationships help us develop an outgoing personality which helps us avoid self-centeredness.

The practical implementation of these relationships must give proper place to holiness, love, wisdom, and ideals. When the building materials are properly applied to the right framework on the right foundation, the building will pass inspection.

5 The Old and New Covenant Approaches to Ethics

Introduction

A. It Is the Difference Between Immaturity and Maturity
1. Under the Old Covenant, God Viewed His People as Children—Thus Immature
2. Under the New Covenant, God Views His People as Being Adults—Thus Mature

B. It Is Primarily a Matter of Method
1. The Method of the Old Covenant Was Adapted to Immaturity
2. The Method of the New Covenant Is Adapted to Maturity

C. The Basic Difference Is Seen in the New Covenant Concept of Stewardship
1. The Old Covenant Believers Are Never Called Stewards
2. The New Covenant Believers Are Called Stewards

INTRODUCTION

It is interesting to observe that what has been said up to this chapter is as pertinent to a Christian approach to psychology and sociology as it is to a study of Christian ethics. Christian truth arises out of theological foundation. It is not developed by taking a non-Christian viewpoint and correcting it by Biblical authority. This is not to say that we cannot receive help in these areas from the labors of those who are not Christians. I do intend to say that we must build on our own foundation. We dare not just improvise what others have prepared.

In our study of ethics, we have given attention to the foundation, the building materials, and the framework. The responsibility before us now is to discover the proper approach to building the structure on the framework from the building materials. The first step in preparing for this approach is to examine the difference between living under the Old and New Covenants.

The basic development in the history of redemption is seen in the main covenants of the Bible. The Edenic Covenant in Genesis 3:15 is the first promise of redemption. There is very little elaboration on the promise. The basic redemptive covenant is the Abrahamic Covenant. In this covenant God promised righteousness and eternal life to the seed of Abraham on the condition of faith (Genesis 13:15; 15:6; 17:8). All of the subsequent covenants in one way or another are involved in preparing for or implementing the Abrahamic Covenant. The New Covenant which was made by Christ with the seed of Abraham is bringing to pass and will bring to pass the fulfilling of the Abrahamic Covenant.

The Mosaic Covenant (or Covenant of Law) which was made with Israel at Mount Sinai is now called the Old Covenant. The Old Covenant served until Christ (Galatians 3:19). Since Christ, the people of God have been delivered from the Old Covenant and are now living under the New Covenant. It is the replacement of the Covenant of Law by the New Covenant that gives to the Covenant of Law the name Old Covenant (Hebrews 8:13).

The replacement of the Covenant of Law with the New Covenant marked a definite change in the way God communicates ethical truth to the believer. To recognize this change is very important in a study of ethics.

A. IT IS THE DIFFERENCE
BETWEEN IMMATURITY AND MATURITY

Under the Old Covenant God Viewed His People as Children—Thus Immature. In Galatians 3:6-18 Paul had established the fact that faith had been made the unchangeable condition of being declared righteous by God and receiving the promise of God. He made it clear that the receiving of the law, which was considerably later than the Abrahamic Covenant, could not change the condition from faith to law-keeping.

If law-keeping could not bring salvation, a logical question is: "Wherefore then serveth the law?" (Galatians 3:19). Paul explains that the law had a temporary purpose. It was to serve "till the seed [Christ] should come" (3:19). It was a moral instructor for the people who lived under it. It made them aware of the true nature of sin and their own lack of righteousness.

Paul gets to the heart of the matter in Galatians 3:23 and 24. In verse 23 there is an article in the Greek before the word *faith*. This would make it read, "But before the faith came." In most places where "the" appears before the word *faith* in the Greek, it refers to the body of truth in which one believes. Faith without the article refers to the experience of believing, while "the faith" refers to what one believes. For example, when Jude says, "Contend for the faith which was once delivered unto the saints" (Jude 3), he is referring to New Covenant truth. It is my personal viewpoint that just as "the law" frequently means the Covenant of Law, "the faith" frequently means the New Covenant. The basic principle of the Covenant of Law is law, while the basic principle of the New Covenant is faith.

Working on the assumption that "the faith" refers to the New Covenant, Galatians 3:23 would read: "But before the New Covenant came, we were kept [guarded, protected] under the law, shut up unto [until] the New Covenant which should afterwards be revealed."

Verse 24 sheds further light on the "kept [or guarded] under the law" of verse 23. It explains "Wherefore [so that] the law was our schoolmaster."

The Greek word which is translated schoolmaster is *paidagogos*. This word is made up of two words, one meaning "child" and the other meaning "leader."

The "child leader" or "child conductor" was a slave who was placed in charge of Greek and Roman boys of wealthy families from the age of 6-7 to the age of 16-17. It was his responsibility to watch over the boy's safety and behavior. When the boy became of age, he was released from the care of the *paidagogos*.

Paul deliberately chose the metaphor of the *paidagogos* to illustrate the ministry of the law. The *paidagogos* was in charge of the boy while he was a child. The ministry of the *paidagogos* was adapted to the immaturity of the child. Paul is telling us by the use of the word *paidagogos* to describe the ministry of the law that God viewed his people as children during the ministry of the law. The law was adapted to their immaturity.

It will be observed that the words *to bring us* are in italics in our Bibles. This was the translators' way of telling us that there were no Greek words from which these words were translated. The translators added them because they thought the addition would make the verse clearer. In most cases, they serve this purpose. Since there are no Greek words for these, we have a right to read the verse without them. The word *unto* may have either a temporal meaning or a spatial meaning. I think the temporal meaning is preferred here.

With the above observations in mind verse 24 would read, "Wherefore the law was our child leader until Christ, that we might be justified by faith." The justified by faith in this verse would refer to the justification of believers by faith during the time they were under the law. That Old Covenant believers were justified by faith was well established by Paul in Galatians 3:6-18.

There is additional proof in Galatians 4:3 that God viewed the Old Covenant believers as children. In Galatians 4:1, 2 Paul gives an illustration. In 4:3-7 he applies the illustration.

Paul explains in 4:1, 2, "Now I say, That the heir, as long as he is a child [under legal age], differeth nothing from a servant [he is under authority like a servant], though he be lord of all; But is under tutors [guardians of his person] and governors [guardians of his estate] until the time appointed of the father [the time he would be considered old enough to be released from the tutors and governors]." The tutors and governors would compare with the *paidagogos* of 3:24.

In verse 3 Paul takes the first step in the application of the illustration. "Even so we, when we were children, were in bondage under the elements of the world." It is clear in the context that Paul is talking about the time when God's people were under the law. He clearly refers to them as "children." "The elements of the world" refers to an elementary system of teaching moral and spiritual truth which was adapted to their immaturity.

Under the New Covenant, God Views His People as Being Adults—Thus Mature. After having pointed out in

Galatians 3:24 that the people of God were under the *paidagogos*, or child leader, until Christ, Paul discusses the release from the *paidagogos* in 3:25. The word *that* in 3:25 is a translation of the Greek article. We may translate: "But after the faith [the New Covenant] is come, we are no longer under a *paidagogos*."

When the Greek and Roman boys were about 16-17, they were considered mature enough to be released from the *paidagogos*. It is quite obvious that Paul is telling us that this is what happened to the people of God when the New Covenant was established by Christ with God's people. Under the New Covenant, we are not under the *paidagogos*. God is now dealing with us on the level of maturity.

Galatians 3:26 is of further interest in the development of this thought. The word *children* is a translation of the Greek word which is most frequently translated "son." Paul gives the word *son* a special meaning in this passage. The son is released from the *paidagogos*. He is treated as mature.

It will also be observed that the word *faith* in 3:26 has the article in the Greek. This tells us that this sonship is ours through the New Covenant. The "in Christ" of this verse is "in union with Christ." The verse would read in the light of these observations: "For ye are all the mature sons of God through the New Covenant in union with Christ."

The idea of viewing God's people in the New Covenant as mature sons of God is further substantiated by Paul's use of the word adoption. It was pointed out

74

above that in Galatians 4:1, 2 Paul gives an illustration. He applies the illustration in 4:3-7. In verse 3 he applies the illustration to the people of God before Christ came. They were children—thus immature.

In 4:4, 5 Paul takes another step in the application of the illustration. He points out that "when the fulness of the time was come, God sent forth his Son." It is obvious that "the fulness of the time" relates to "the time appointed of the father" in the illustration. This was the time when the father had set for the heir to be freed from the tutors and governors. He was to be released from a treatment adapted to immaturity and enter into the freedom of maturity.

The fullness of time of 4:4 refers to the time when God chose to release His people from the treatment adapted to immaturity, as was the case with the law. He was ready to start dealing with His people on a level adapted to maturity. When this time had come, He sent His Son to bring about this new relationship.

The purpose of Christ's coming as stated in verse 5 was twofold: (1) "To [the Greek reads 'that he might'] redeem them that were under the law." This would refer to salvation from the curse of the law, (compare this with Galatians 3:13). (2) "That we might receive the adoption of sons." The Greek word which is translated "adoption of sons" means "son-placing." The idea here is that we might be placed in the position of a son. The son-placing would take place at the time appointed of the father in the illustration in 4:1, 2. This would be a time of release from the tutors and governors.

75

The development of thought in Galatians 4:1-5 makes it clear that adoption, or son-placing, is not used the same way here that it is in our society. It does not refer to taking one who is not a member of a family and making him a member of the family. Rather, it refers to taking one who is a member of a family and placing him in the position of a mature son. This introduces him to the freedom and responsibility of maturity, and means that he will no longer be treated on the level of a child.

This thought of considering the word *son* to refer to a mature son is further substantiated by 4:7. Paul says, "Wherefore thou art no more a servant, but a son." This refers back to the illustration again. In the illustration it is said that "the heir, as long as he is a child [under legal age], differeth nothing from a servant" (4:1). In verse 7 the comparison of the heir with a servant is no longer valid. Why is it no longer valid? He is a son. Being a son means that he is delivered from the childhood method of treatment.

The point is clear. Under the New Covenant we are delivered from the Mosaic Law. The way God communicates ethical truth and the way we receive it is in keeping with the position of maturity now enjoyed by the people of God.

It is important that we recognize that when we are considered mature, this is in contrast to the Old Covenant believers. In our own personal experiences, the new convert would be immature in contrast to a mature Christian. All Christians are mature in contrast to the Old Covenant believers. Only those who have

developed through growth are mature in contrast to the
new convert.

B. IT IS PRIMARILY A MATTER OF METHOD

Having established the fact that God viewed His
people under the Old Covenant as immature and His
people under the New Covenant as mature, we will now
move on to the practical implications of this difference.
We are told in Galatians 3:19—4:7 that God views us
now as mature in contrast to the immaturity under the
Old Covenant. For the most part, the practical implications of this difference have to be observed from an
inductive study of the Old and New Testaments
(Covenants).

**The Method of the Old Covenant Was Adapted to
Immaturity.** A study of the Old Covenant laws reveals
that stress was placed on the objective and the tangible.
Numerous laws were written out. (See Exodus
21:1—23:19.) The priesthood with its system of sacrifices made considerable use of what we might call object
lessons.

The application of the principles of moral law was
given in detail in the civil laws. The principle of
repetition is seen in the repeated offering of sacrifices
and the feast-days which were repeated every year.

It is obvious that there is a parallel to be found in
the way God dealt with His people under the law and
the way we deal with children. Instructions have to be

spelled out in detail for children. They need to be reminded again and again what they should and should not do. Considerable use is made of object lessons in teaching children.

The Method of the New Covenant Is Adapted to Maturity. A comparison between the Old and New Covenants makes it obvious that there are far fewer specific instructions in the New Covenant than were found in the Old Covenant. The New Covenant places stress on principles and attitudes. One does not need to commit an act to sin. His heart attitude can make him guilty (Matthew 5:27, 28; 1 John 3:15). On the other hand, good actions not accompanied by the right attitude are not adequate (1 Corinthians 13:3).

In the Old Covenant the sacrificial system was a divinely instituted system of object lessons. In the New Testament the ordinances are the only divinely instituted object lessons.

As children grow older there is a decrease in the specified number of "do's" and "don'ts." More reliance is made on principles and heart attitude. Less use is made of the visible to teach the invisible. That these changes have been made from the Old Covenant to the New Covenant is abundantly clear. God deals with us on a more mature plane than He did with Old Covenant believers.

There is no change in the basic moral ideals and concerns that Christian parents have for their children when they are small than when they grow up. There is a difference in the way they communicate these truths.

The same can be said about the way God communicated moral and spiritual truth in the Old and New Covenants. The basic truth is the same. The specific application as it was adapted to the immaturity of the Old Covenant believer may change for the New Covenant believer.

Parents will warn a two-year-old of numerous dangers in the yard and will not let him leave the yard. After much counsel about danger and how to cross the street, they will let a six-year-old venture a short distance away from the house in familiar territory. As the child grows older, he will reach the point he is only reminded to be careful. The specifics of communication change, but the basic concept of safety is the true concern throughout.

In the Old Covenant, if a person stole an ox and killed it or sold it, he was to restore five for one. If it were a sheep, he was to restore four for one (Exodus 22:1). The basic principle is restitution. The principle of restitution would be an abiding principle. The five for one in the case of an ox and the four for one in the case of a sheep would not be in force today. This illustrates how the basic truth in the Old Covenant laws is abiding, but the specifics are not unless they are inseparable from the basic truth.

Some have said that we are delivered from the civil laws and the ceremonial laws, but not from the moral laws in the Ten Commandments. This is not the best way to explain the deliverance from law. We are delivered from a system of laws in which laws are the basic method of teaching ethical truth. We are delivered from the method of law, but not from the basic truth in the law. The basic truth found in the civil laws, ceremonial laws, and the Ten Commandments is eternal. We are not delivered from the basic truths in either of these divisions of the law. The morality of the Ten Commandments is stated in such basic form that it is brought into the New Covenant in the same form. The same is not true of the civil laws and the ceremonial laws, but we are still bound by the basic truth taught in these laws.

In the Old Covenant the sin-offering taught the basic truth of the need of a substitute to pay for sin. We need a substitute to pay for our sins, but we do not have to offer the animal sacrifice which taught this truth. We simply trust in Jesus Christ who offered himself as our sin-offering.

Children must be taught in a way suited for children. To try to apply the same approach to adults has tragic results. The Old Covenant was good for the people at the time they were under it. It was adapted to their immaturity. The new approach is better for us. It is adapted to our maturity. We must acquaint ourselves with the basic approach to New Covenant ethics and follow it. The results of trying to use the Old Covenant approach of a system of laws would be tragic for us. In the New Covenant we have moral laws, but we do not have a system of laws.

A written law furnishes dogmatic proof that a matter is either right or wrong. The absence of a system of laws in the New Covenant means that we cannot always offer dogmatic proof. If this were the case, the New Covenant would simply be a replacement of one system of laws by another system of laws. We are delivered from the method of law, not just from the Mosaic system of laws. To demand dogmatic proof for our ethical decisions is to miss the meaning of deliverance from the law.

It should be observed that deliverance from the law as we have discussed it is not the same as deliverance from the curse of the law. The sinner is under the curse of the law. The Christian is not. The deliverance from the law as we have studied it is historical. The Old Covenant believer was dealt with through the Mosaic Law. The New Covenant believer is delivered from the Mosaic Law. This deliverance is from the method of law, not just the Mosaic Law.

C. THE BASIC DIFFERENCE IS SEEN IN THE NEW COVENANT CONCEPT OF STEWARDSHIP

The Old Covenant Believers Are Never Called Stewards. The word *steward* is found in the Old Covenant, but only in the literal sense. It is not used metaphorically in referring to the believers. The development of the concept of stewardship below will make it clear that the Old Covenant believer did not have the latitude that is necessary to develop the full implications of stewardship in his life.

The New Covenant Believers Are Called Stewards.

The word that is translated "steward" in the New Testament referred to one who was over an estate. He was accountable to the owner, but he was the manager of the estate. He had a planning responsibility. He did not simply carry out a list of orders. He had to think and plan.

In the New Covenant we are said to be stewards of our gifts and callings (1 Peter 4:10; Titus 1:7). We are stewards of the mysteries of God (1 Corinthians 4:1, 2). We are stewards of the gospel (1 Corinthians 9:17; Ephesians 3:2). The word translated "dispensation" in these verses is the Greek word for stewardship.

This thinking and planning responsibility with accountability to God for our stewardship gets at the very heart of what it means to be a New Covenant believer. This thinking and planning responsibility goes into the area of ethics. We are responsible to take the few moral laws given in the New Covenant and the moral principles taught and apply them to the situations of life. We are accountable for what we do.

In the Old Covenant they were told more and less was expected because of their immaturity. In the New Covenant we are told less and more is expected because of our maturity.

6 | Basic Principles in Studying Ethical Truth

Introduction
A. Reason, Biblical Authority, and the Holy Spirit Must Each Be Given Proper Place
   1. Reason Must Be Used
   2. The Authority of the Bible Must Be Recognized
   3. The Ministry of the Holy Spirit Must Be Recognized
B. The Inner Nature of Man Must Be Taken into Account
   1. Man Is Morally Constituted
   2. Moral Knowledge Is for the Whole Person
C. The Proper Value of Righteousness Must Be Seen
   1. Sin Must Be Viewed as Bad
   2. Righteousness Must Be Seen as Good
D. Honesty Must Be Followed
   1. Honesty Is Committed to Truth
   2. Honesty Is Committed to the Conviction that Truth Is Good

INTRODUCTION

In the previous chapter, it was observed that as New Covenant believers we are viewed as mature. We have a stewardship responsibility. We are to think and plan. In the area of ethics, God has given us a few basic laws and principles. He has not given us a detailed list of laws that describe our ethical responsibility in every situation of life. It is our personal responsibility as stewards to take the basic laws and principles and apply them to life situations. There are a few basic principles that must be followed in our pursuit of ethical knowledge for life situations.

A. REASON, BIBLICAL AUTHORITY, AND THE HOLY SPIRIT MUST BE GIVEN PROPER PLACE

We cannot settle for the approach: "I am a Christian. God will let me know when I do wrong." Certainly, God is good to us in helping us when we truly seek the right answers about right and wrong, and good and bad. However, to expect God to impress some idea on our minds, make us feel bad, or bring some kind of difficulty in our lives every time we do wrong is overlooking the fact that we have a stewardship responsibility.

Reason Must Be Used. Man is rational as a result of being made in the image of God. The development of this rationality is a divine obligation. Reason came not as a product of the fall, but as a product of creation.

A fear regarding the use of the mind has always been prevalent in the Church. Some have taken the Biblical statements about the wrong use of reason to mean that reason is bad. It is the wrong use of reason that is bad, not reason itself.

Paul explains that reason without revelation did not lead man to God (1 Corinthians 1:21). First Corinthians 2:9 tells us that spiritual truth is not discovered through science and philosophy. First Corinthians 2:10 tells us that the source of spiritual truth is revelation.

To say that reason is not the author of our view of God is not to say that our faith in revealed truth is not reasonable. There is nothing that makes more sense than believing in God, but our conviction of God's existence and our view of God are not the product of a set of proofs. Man is never more rational than when he believes in God.

Proverbs 3:5, 6 creates a problem for some in the use of reason. However, the statement, "Lean not unto thine own understanding," cannot be taken to mean that the Christian is to set his mind aside. To understand it to mean this would be to miss the basic thrust of the Book of Proverbs which gives a strong emphasis to wisdom, knowledge, and understanding.

A proper interpretation of "thine own understanding" would be an understanding that leaves God and the Bible out of the picture. We are to avoid dependence upon such understanding. But we are to place a high value on an understanding that acknowledges God and takes into account the moral and spiritual truth revealed in the Bible.

The Bible gives a positive place to the use of the mind. We are to love God with our minds (Matthew 22:37). We are to be fully persuaded in our minds (Romans 14:5). God will put His laws in our minds (Hebrews 8:10). We are told to give "an answer to every man that asketh you a reason of the hope that is in you" (1 Peter 3:15).

We must not, in our pursuit of ethical knowledge, allow ourselves to be guided by reasoning that fails to be guided by a recognition of God and the Bible. Yet, we must use our minds. The very idea of a Christian system of ethics arises out of the idea that man is rational. There can be no ethical knowledge apart from the use of the mind. We must *think* if we are to understand the application of right and wrong, or good and bad, to the various situations of life.

The Authority of the Bible Must Be Recognized. The Bible is the Christian's basic source book on ethics. It is an infallible authority "for correction, for instruction in righteousness" (2 Timothy 3:16). The psalmist considered the written Word to be a light to his moral and spiritual pathway (Psalm 119:105).

The Bible furnishes the material for a system of ethics, but it is not given in systematic form. The Bible furnishes laws and principles that are adequate for every situation of life, but it does not show their application to every situation of life.

The truth of the Bible is at times given in formulated statements of truth. Much of the Bible is the history of men and their experiences with God. In this history we see truth as it encounters human experience.

We must study both the formulated statements of truth and the experience of men with God. For example, we gain an added dimension of the judgment of God, when we not only read the statements on God's judgment, but also read about the acts of God's judgment recorded in Scripture.

In 1 Corinthians 6:18 Paul said, "Flee fornication." The truth is clear from the statement, but it aids us in bringing truth and life together when we read the accounts of Joseph and David. We see the positive example of Joseph as he flees fornication when tempted by Potiphar's wife (Genesis 39). Joseph kept his purity. He suffered for it for a while, but he was rewarded in the long run.

David's experience with Bathsheba is an example of the tragedy that befell one who did not flee fornication. For a moment of pleasure David brought judgment and misery into his life and into his family.

The highest point in God's revelation is seen in the birth, life, ministry, death, burial, and resurrection of Jesus Christ. In Jesus we see truth and life brought together. Jesus taught by both precept and practice. He taught righteousness and lived righteousness. He taught love and lived love.

We are far better off by having formulated statements of truth interwoven with the experiences of men with God than we would have been with an organized, systematic presentation of truth. If the Bible had been a systematic presentation of truth, no doubt many points would not have been so debatable. However, it is far better to see truth coming together with human experience than it is to be able to settle minor points in a debate.

In our study of the Bible, we must seek to formulate statements of ethical truth. We need objective statements. Without objective authority, we are left at the mercy of the changing winds of time. We must also labor to address life with this objective truth. Truth must be experienced in the arena of life.

The Ministry of the Holy Spirit Must Be Recognized. The Holy Spirit is deeply concerned with righteousness. It appears that He bears the name Holy Spirit because His basic responsibility is to produce holiness in us. He is the Spirit of Truth (John 16:13). As the Spirit of Truth, He guides us in our pursuit of ethical truth. "He will reprove the world of sin, and of righteousness, and of judgment" (John 16:8).

The question that concerns us is: How does the Holy Spirit guide us into ethical truth? Does He always say to us, in some way, when we face an ethical decision, "This is right or this is wrong?" Or does He always say after we commit a sin, "You did wrong?"

Let us suppose that the answer to the above questions would be "yes." What would be the implications of such a position? There would be no need of

Bible study on matters of right and wrong. There would be no need of thinking on such matters. There would be no need of a study of ethics. In fact a study of the Bible and the use of the mind would be risky. If the Holy Spirit always tells us what is right and what is wrong, we would do better not to confuse ourselves with studying the Bible to find out about right and wrong.

Certainly, the Holy Spirit is good to us in helping us to understand what is right and what is wrong. However, His ministry is not intended to undercut the importance of studying the Bible which He inspired. Our understanding of the ministry of the Holy Spirit must take into account the authority of the Bible and the responsibility of the Christian to use his mind.

We cannot fully understand the ministry of the Holy Spirit. There is a mystical aspect of His work that defies explanation. One would gather from Scripture that at times the Holy Spirit makes a direct impression upon the mind of the believer (Acts 13:2; 16:6, 7). Our own experiences tell us that at times we believe that God is impressing us to take or not to take a certain path of action. At times we have the feeling that the Holy Spirit is reminding us that a certain path of action is wrong.

For the most part, we do not feel that the Holy Spirit gives us a direct impression concerning what we should do in every situation of life. Much of what we do is determined by our understanding of the Bible, and what sanctified common sense would tell us is appropriate.

We must not view the Bible, the Holy Spirit, and our mind as being isolated from each other. Rather, we must view our whole Christian experience as being in the context of being indwelt by the Holy Spirit. The Holy Spirit aids us when we study the Bible. He aids us as we use common sense to apply the principles of the Bible to life situations. Wisdom is a gift of the Holy Spirit (1 Corinthians 12:8).

The ministry of the Holy Spirit does not always take the form of a conscious impression in helping us understand the Bible and its application to life. It is a mistake to limit the ministry of the Holy Spirit to conscious impressions. For the most part the work of the Holy Spirit in us takes the form of an overshadowing and a working through the thought processes on the unconscious, or somewhat unconscious, level. As Christians, we can look back and clearly see the hand of God in various decisions that we made. Yet in many cases we were not consciously aware that God was impressing us to make the decision when we made it. We trusted in God to help us. We did what we thought was appropriate. Yet as we look back we see more than our unaided ability in the decision. We see the hand of God at work.

At this point it will be helpful to recall that God has made us persons. A person is one who thinks, feels, and acts. The Holy Spirit does not look at us as puppets to be manipulated. To do so would defeat the purpose of God in making us persons. The Holy Spirit is a person. Each of us is a person. The Holy Spirit views us as persons to be motivated and influenced. He sees us as being deeply involved in our own learning process, yet dependent upon Him for help.

There is no contradiction between dependence upon the Holy Spirit, and the recognition of the infallible authority of the Bible, and the active use of our minds in the pursuit of truth. We must never make it a choice between depending upon the Holy Spirit or the use of our minds. We must depend upon the Holy Spirit *while* using our minds. If we should ever feel that the Holy Spirit is leading us to do something against the teaching of the Scriptures, we must take the position that it is not the Holy Spirit leading us. Such feelings are either from our own sinful promptings, or they are from Satan.

B. THE INNER NATURE OF MAN MUST BE TAKEN INTO ACCOUNT

Man Is Morally Constituted. The quest for moral knowledge is no more optional with man than his quest for food and water. We cannot ignore the fact that we are moral. Concern about right and wrong is so deeply placed into our being that it cannot be eradicated. Those who do not want to accept moral responsibility will suffer the consequences.

The words of Isaiah are well spoken when he said, "Woe unto them that call evil good, and good evil; that put darkness for light, and light for darkness; that put bitter for sweet, and sweet for bitter!" (Isaiah 5:20).

The woe is not limited to a divinely inflicted penalty at the final judgment nor to some calamity in their life. The woe is an internal suffering that comes to one who tries to cope with the moral issue by simply changing the labels.

What we need is truth. Jesus said, "And ye shall know the truth, and the truth shall make you free" (John 8:32).

Moral Knowledge Is for the Whole Person. Moral knowledge is for the heart and will, not merely the mind. It is for life. It can never be merely academic. We cannot, so-to-speak, stand on the outside and study moral truth as an uninvolved onlooker. We cannot be neutral. We must study as a committed person.

A half-hearted interest in moral truth blinds the eyes of the searcher to the truth. Twenty-twenty vision in moral truth can be approached only by those who love God with their entire being, love their neighbor as themselves, and have a proper appreciation for the created order.

Moral truth must be learned in conflict. In spite of the fact that moral truth is a must for our own good, we must deal with opposition within ourselves. There is conflict from others, and there is conflict from Satan.

Only the dedicated win in warfare. The half-hearted figure is not worth it. They see the comforts of compromise. Only those who mean business with God will be able to see beyond the most obvious morality of the Ten Commandments.

C. THE PROPER VALUE
OF RIGHTEOUSNESS MUST BE SEEN

Sin Must Be Viewed as Bad. Even among those who recognize that sin is wrong, many have been deceived into thinking that sin is good (not good in the sense of being right, but good in the sense of offering happiness). Many have felt that righteousness is a wet blanket that takes pleasure out of living. They think that righteousness is for those who have reached a point in life that they can resign themselves to a dull, boring, uneventful life. It is felt that sin would really be the happy life if God were not against it. Since God is the judge before whom we must ultimately stand, it is thought that it will be better to do right and live an unhappy life here than to live a happy life in sin here and go to Hell in the hereafter.

We must not buy the devil's propaganda that sin is more enjoyable than righteousness. We are made for righteousness. Sin is a poisonous diet that will lead to serious malfunction in this life and damnation in the life to come. Sin is like ocean water to thirsty man on a life raft. At first it is pleasant, but then it leads to serious consequences. To drink is to sacrifice the future on the altar of the immediate. Such a decision is the choice of one the Bible calls a fool.

Sin offers quick thrills. It offers excitement and elation immediately. Sexual immorality, alcohol, and drugs offer moments of pleasure. The problem is that the pleasure lasts no longer than the experience. Every memory of sin is an unpleasant memory. Sin robs a person of self-respect. There can be no happiness without self-respect. The person who has let sin take away his self-respect may become a victim of depression and despair. His level of enjoyment sinks to the base and the forbidden. He hangs on from one thrill with sin to another thrill with sin.

There are others who have not as yet fallen so low in their depression and despair. With them life is a game. They play hard to keep from thinking about themselves. They may play music so loud they cannot think about themselves. They may have a compulsion to be with a crowd. They cannot stand to be alone. They must be entertained all the time. The responsibilities of life are drudgery.

When we see sin for what it is, we see it as bad, not good. Paul has well described sin as exceeding sinful (Romans 7:13). To be happy, we must detect sin and shun it.

Righteousness Must Be Seen as Good. Righteousness is the diet for which man is designed. It is the foundation of self-respect. In a world of conflict, it may sometimes be hard to do right. One may suffer ridicule. He may be confronted with sin's offer of quick thrills which he must resist. Sometimes the going may be tough, but the one who stands steadfastly for righteousness is building self-respect. When the battle is over, the harder we had to fight to win the better we feel about the victory. There is a clean feeling when we do right.

Every memory of righteousness is a pleasant memory. The person who cheats on an examination may feel a temporary sense of relief, but he has haunting memories. The person who refuses to cheat may feel bad about not making a higher grade, but he has pleasant memories about his refusal to cheat. The couple who fall into sin in courtship may have a moment of pleasure, but they look back with sorrow on the event. The couple who behaved properly during courtship can look back with pleasant memories as long as they live.

Some try to cope with sin by changing the label and calling the sin they want to perform right. The person who does so is forever having to justify his deed. The person who practices sexual immorality is forever having to defend his actions. Those who practice purity do not have to defend the rightness of purity. Label-changing will never suffice for righteous living.

Righteousness is not designed to give quick thrills —like intoxication with alcohol or a trip on drugs. It is designed to give deep, lasting peace and satisfaction that makes temporary thrills through illegitimate means unnecessary. There are exciting moments in the Christian life, but the thing that really counts is how things are between the moments of excitement. The person who practices righteousness welcomes legitimate thrills and excitement, but his world does not come to an end when they are not available. He is sustained by the permanent experience of peace, satisfaction, and contentment.

Jesus said, "Blessed [happy] are they which do hunger and thirst after righteousness: for they shall be filled" (Matthew 5:6). This happiness is based on the fact that righteousness is not only right, but good.

Hungering and thirsting after righteousness is a must for the one who is in the pursuit of ethical truth. It is only when we see that sin is bad and righteousness is good that we will have the right attitude toward righteousness. It is only then that we will be able to truly desire to recognize sin so we can forsake it, and recognize righteousness so we can practice it.

D. HONESTY MUST BE FOLLOWED

Honesty Is Committed to Truth. Usually when we think of honesty, we think of telling the truth. Honesty, also, requires one to believe the truth and reject error. Honesty is a prejudice toward truth without regard for consequences.

Honesty in thought is what people have in mind when they speak about being objective. In my opinion, to be objective is not what we should set forth as the ideal in seeking the truth. Objectivity indicates that a person sees himself as being detached from the subject under study. Or, he seeks to act and think like one who is detached. Does detachment or lack of involvement make one a better judge of truth than one who is involved?

Is not the ideal an involved person who is

disciplined by honesty? He makes his feelings bow to truth when the evidence is against his feelings. If one cannot so discipline his feelings, he cannot be an accurate judge of truth. Maybe an uninvolved person can at times make pertinent observations, but there is an insight that the involved person has that will not be seen by the uninvolved and unconcerned person.

One of the reasons that so much theological literature does not speak to people is that the theologian had objectivity as his goal. He wrote as a detached person. In so doing, he detached the truth he was writing from life. We cannot be neutral observers in our study of ethics. We study as one who is deeply involved and deeply concerned. We seek to be honest, but not detached.

Honesty takes all pertinent data into account. No data is deliberately avoided. Final judgment is suspended when the data is inadequate. Adjustments in position are made if new data should require it.

Honesty Is Committed to the Conviction that Truth Is Good. It takes a deep commitment to truth for one to be honest to the point of actually desiring truth. Prejudice toward our own ideas may be so deep that it is hard to be honest when we see them shaken. The commitment to honesty works on the assumption that truth is not only right, but good (John 8:32). Truth is better than error. Error may at times give temporary success, but in the long run it leads to ruin. Truth pays in the long run.

The assumption that truth and righteousness are

good motivates us toward an honest search for ethical knowledge. The person who practices honesty may not always arrive at truth with his first conclusion, but given time truth will emerge.

7 Christian Liberty

Introduction
A. The New Covenant Teachings on Liberty
   1. The Foundation of the Concept of Christian Liberty
   2. The Basic Idea of Christian Liberty
B. Guiding Principles in the Exercise of Liberty
   1. Liberty, Not License
   2. Love for Others
   3. Concern for Testimony and Influence
C. Conclusion

INTRODUCTION

The doctrine of Christian liberty grows out of the fact that the New Covenant believer has been placed in the position of a mature son as was pointed out in chapter 5. This involved deliverance from God's method of treatment adapted to immaturity.

In looking back at the time God's people were

99

under the law, Paul referred to them as being "in bondage under the elements of the world" (Galatians 4:3). Concerning our position as New Covenant believers, Paul said, "Stand fast therefore in the liberty wherewith Christ hath made us free, and be not entangled again with the yoke of bondage" (Galatians 5:1).

It is important for us to get a proper concept of Christian liberty. On the one hand there are those who suppress the doctrine of Christian liberty out of fear that it will lead to sinning. On the other hand there are those who interpret the doctrine of Christian liberty in such a manner that it results in an anemic morality. Neither of these approaches is a proper grasp of the teachings of the New Covenant.

A. THE NEW COVENANT TEACHING ON LIBERTY

The Foundation of the Concept of Christian Liberty. Jesus' teaching prepared the way for the New Covenant approach to ethics. The whole New Testament in its ethical teachings is consistent with the doctrine of Christian liberty. The basic development and elaboration of the doctrine is found in the writings of Paul.

Paul applies the doctrine of liberty in other books, but the basic idea is found in Galatians. "The liberty wherewith Christ hath made us free" is contrasted with "the yoke of bondage" of the Old Covenant believer (Galatians 5:1).

It is important to observe that the bondage of Galatians 5:1 is not the bondage of condemnation. When Paul is discussing the deliverance from the bondage of the law, he is not speaking of deliverance from the curse of the law. The New Covenant believer is delivered from the law in two ways: (1) He is delivered from the curse of the law. (2) He is delivered from the law as the *paidagogos* which was a child conductor (see chapter 5).

Deliverance from the curse of the law means deliverance from the obligation to pay the penalty. This deliverance was accomplished by Jesus Christ when He was made a curse for us (Galatians 3:13). While the actual work of delivering believers from the curse of the law was accomplished at Calvary, the Old Covenant believers experienced freedom from the obligation to pay the penalty for their sins. They were forgiven on the basis of the payment of the penalty that would be made by Christ on their behalf. If this had not been the case, there would have been no salvation for anyone under the Old Covenant.

When we think of New Covenant believers being delivered from the law in a way differing from Old Covenant believers, we are not referring to deliverance from the curse of the law. We must not think of Old Covenant believers as being saved by law-keeping while New Covenant believers are saved by grace. Salvation has always been by grace. It is true that the concept of grace is seen more clearly by New Covenant believers, but the fact of salvation by grace is as old as salvation.

101

There never was salvation without grace.

The deliverance from the law which relates to the liberty of the New Covenant believer is deliverance from the law as the *paidagogos*. It is deliverance from a childhood method of treatment. The experience of being under the law-method is called *bondage* because of its detailed instructions and its ceremonial obligations. It did not leave as much freedom to the person.

The New Covenant position is called *liberty* in contrast to its bondage of being under the *paidagogos*. God uses a different approach to communicating moral and spiritual truth to the New Covenant believer. We have revealed to us a few basic laws and basic principles. We have the liberty to exercise personal responsibility in applying these principles to life situations.

It is important to observe that neither deliverance from the curse of the law, nor deliverance from the law, as *paidagogos*, means that law is completely set aside. Deliverance from the curse of the law means that the law no longer pronounces a curse upon disobedience. Perfect obedience is not required from us for justification. We are justified by Christ's perfect obedience and death. To say that law cannot pronounce a curse upon the believer is not to say that moral law cannot instruct the believer. It does not mean that the believer no longer has moral responsibility.

The design of salvation is to make us holy. Salvation is for those who want to be forgiven of their sins and made holy. It is inconceivable that a person who wants to be holy would have anything other than the highest regard for moral law.

Deliverance from the law, as *paidagogos*, is a deliverance not from law as such, but law as revealed in the Mosaic Law. In the Mosaic Law, we have a system of law. Law is the basic method of communicating ethical truth.

The law-method served a temporary need in the history of the people of God. It was indispensable during the period of the immaturity of the people of God. However, the law-method was inadequate for a permanent means of expressing ethical truth.

The inadequacy of the law-method is seen in its tendency toward formalism and legalism. It tends toward abuse in producing outward conformity that does not come from a proper heart attitude. The prophets cried out against outward obedience that did not come from the heart. In delivering the Word of God Isaiah said, "Your new moons and your appointed feasts my soul hateth: they are a trouble unto me; I am weary to bear them" (Isaiah 1:14).

The failure of the law-method reached its low in Pharisaism. The Pharisees went far beyond the Mosaic Law. They sought to spell out every responsibility of life in terms of a law. This was done through oral tradition, or what the New Testament calls the tradition of the elders (Matthew 15:2). It was Jesus' unwillingness to accept the law-method as a framework for ethical truth that brought such fierce conflict between Him and the Pharisees.

Deliverance from the law, as the *paidagogos*, not

only delivered from the Mosiac Law; it also delivered God's people from the law-method. This is not the same as thinking of total deliverance from moral law. There is moral law in the New Covenant. There are moral laws. All the Ten Commandments, except the Sabbath Commandment, are quoted in the New Testament as having moral authority. A number of things are referred to as being sin (Romans 1:29-32; 1 Corinthians 6:9, 10; Galatians 5:19-21; Ephesians 5:3-6).

While there are laws in the New Covenant, it is noticeably obvious that the list is not nearly so complete as in the Old Covenant. Basic truths and basic principles are taught, but it is left up to believers to apply them to life-situations. The liberty of the New Covenant believer is in keeping with his position of maturity.

Both the Old Covenant believers and the New Covenant believers were under grace. They were both delivered from the curse of the law. Both the Old Covenant believer and the New Covenant believer were responsible to obey moral law. Morality was communicated to Old Covenant believers through the law-method. The New Covenant believer is delivered from the law-method. He has more liberty and responsibility.

The Basic Idea of Christian Liberty. The New Covenant doctrine of liberty works on the assumption that not all things are authoritatively settled in terms of a law. There is a responsibility for the individual. Under God, the believer is capable of making valid decisions. This does not guarantee the accuracy of his decisions, but it does guarantee his right to make them. There are no authoritative priests, judges, or prophets whose word is law.

The doctrine of Christian liberty is in keeping with the recognition of our being persons. Christian liberty is God's recognition of the fact that we are thinking, feeling, acting beings. It enables us to develop and mature. The movement of God from Genesis 3:15 to the coming of Christ was working toward the time when God's people could have the liberty and the background for full development as persons.

Paul is addressing the liberty of the New Covenant believer when he said, "Let every man be fully persuaded in his own mind" (Romans 14:5). The Old Covenant had a system of days (Leviticus 23). Paul did not choose to settle the problem by an authoritative statement.

There was the problem in many of the early churches concerning what to eat and what not to eat. Paul said, "For one believeth that he may eat all things: another, who is weak, eateth herbs." His instructions were: "Let not him that eateth despise him that eateth not; and let not him which eateth not judge him that eateth: for God hath received him" (Romans 14:2, 3).

The basic idea involved in Christian liberty is that each believer is capable and responsible, and has the freedom to carry out his responsibility. He is a steward with a planning responsibility. He is not given a detailed set of orders that covers every situation. He is not under authoritative persons whose word is law.

B. GUIDING PRINCIPLES
IN THE EXERCISE OF LIBERTY

Liberty, Not License. The doctrine of liberty has always been subject to abuse. Part of this abuse is more related to the doctrine of grace than to the doctrine of Christian liberty. Since many equate these two doctrines, their misunderstanding of grace comes over into their doctrine of liberty. The logic is that, if Jesus' death and righteousness settled man's account with God, there is no real need of moral concern on the part of the believer. Moral concern may be admirable, but not necessary. Jesus has already settled the account. Sin on our part will not undo it. Following this logic, it is better not to get overly concerned since this concern would interfere with evangelism. It is felt that a morally anemic Christian experience might have more appeal to depraved people.

The view described above is called *antinomianism*. It means *against law*. Its advocates teach that the Christian is not bound by moral law. There have been very few people in the history of the Church that have been thoroughgoing antinomians. However, traces of its influence can be seen in the shallow concern about holiness that grows out of misconception of grace.

It is too clear in Scripture that man is justified by faith alone for it to be questioned. It is clear that salvation is by grace and thus a gift. This will confuse us if we do not pause long enough to discover what salvation is. Salvation consists of both justification and sanctification. In justification, there is the forgiveness of sins. In sanctification there is the change of attitude and experience with sin and holiness. There are two aspects of saving grace: justifying grace and sanctifying grace.

It is true that grace is an unmerited favor, but this unmerited favor involves both justification and sanctification. The person who wants to be saved wants to have his sins forgiven and his experience with sin and holiness changed. He wants to become holy. He cannot receive forgiveness of sins without receiving a changed heart and life. If the person who wants salvation wants to become holy and if sanctification is designed to help him become holy, it is inconceivable that a saved person can have a disregard for holiness. If there is no moral concern, there is no salvation.

Antinomianism is the error that results when justifying grace is not accompanied by sanctifying grace in a person's thought. Justification and sanctification are distinct, but they can never be separated. A person cannot receive one without receiving the other.

A proper understanding of justifying grace is essential to the experience of Christian liberty. We need to see that our justification is not dependent upon our own obedience, but Christ's obedience and death. This puts our experience on a solid foundation. It frees us from the bondage of fear. We can take an honest look at sin. If there is no concern about sin, there is no salvation. On the other hand, those who are concerned about sin do not have to feel it is all over when through weakness they commit a sin.

Another abuse of Christian liberty comes from a false interpretation of the fact that each Christian must make his own decisions with regard to ethical matters. Unless there is a misunderstanding of the doctrine of grace, it is usually conceded that Christian liberty does not permit one to violate the direct teachings of the New Testament. The problem comes in the application of the principles of the New Testament to things not specifically mentioned in the New Testament. There are two basic errors that sometimes are seen in the interpretation of the meaning of the individual's liberty to apply the principles of the New Testament to things not specifically mentioned. (1) Some seem to think that since it is the individual's liberty to make such decisions, whatever decision he makes is right for him. (2) There are those who feel that others have no right to express concern about the decisions a person makes with regard to things not specifically mentioned in the New Testament.

Let us examine the first error. What this amounts to is freedom without accountability. If whatever decision is made is correct, there is no room for accounting for error. The New Covenant believer is not less responsible. He is more responsible. Liberty is not intended to weaken or destroy accountability. It is intended to give freedom to prepare for accountability.

When this freedom is taken to mean that any decision is right for the person making it, it runs the risk of ceasing to be "Christian" liberty. There is a distinction between Christian liberty and absolute liberty.

Absolute liberty is not bound by any framework of thought. Christian liberty is. Christian liberty operates within the framework of a commitment to Christian values and principles. Only those who hunger and thirst after righteousness (Matthew 5:6) can exercise Christian liberty. Only those who recognize sin as being bad and righteousness as being good are in a position to make a valid use of Christian liberty. The liberty exercised by church members who are indifferent to moral and spiritual concerns cannot be recognized as a valid exercise of Christian liberty.

It must be remembered that Christian liberty is not the liberty to do as one pleases in matters not mentioned in the New Testament. It is the liberty for each person to apply the principles of the New Testament to situations not specifically mentioned. This calls for a serious commitment to the principles taught in the New Testament. Failure to be committed to the principles of the New Testament renders one incapable of exercising Christian liberty.

Let us now turn our attention to the second error growing out of a misinterpretation of the liberty of the individual to apply the principle of the New Testament to life situations. Are we required to show no concern for the way another person uses his liberty? Do we have to adopt a hands-off policy? Such an approach would make legalism the only valid approach to ethics in concern for the actions of others. Legalism sees law as the only valid form of expression of ethics. Legalism can take two approaches: (1) Only what is written in the inspired record as law is law. (2) In addition to recognizing the laws in the Bible, we must formulate laws from Biblical principles to express ethical truth.

If our expression of moral concern for our fellow Christians must be limited to the things specifically forbidden or specifically commanded in the New Testament, we have fallen into the trap of the first type of legalism mentioned above. We are saying that we have no right to express concern to anyone except where violation of revealed laws is concerned. We could seek to get them to obey law, but we could not share with them our understanding of the application of principles. Every person would be a law unto himself, without the benefit of the experience of others where application of principle is involved. Such a view would be a gross misunderstanding of the New Testament.

Certainly there must be areas of difference where we respect the opinion of the other person. We must not demand absolute conformity to our own view of things from others. The application of principles to life situations is too complex to expect everyone to see alike on everything. Paul asked those in the church at Rome to respect each other when they differed on the matter of what to eat and what not to eat (Romans 14:3).

When we see people of sincere moral concern have opinions that differ from others, we are to respect them. Where differences grow out of a lack of moral concern, we are to admonish them. It is interesting to note that the specific areas where Paul asked that liberty of opinion be allowed are areas that were not dealing with the liberty of a person to do what Paul considered wrong. The chief issue was the issue of what to eat and what not to eat (Romans 14; 1 Corinthians 8 and 10). Paul took the position that it was all right to eat the meat in question, yet he respected and taught respect for those who thought it was wrong.

The primary thing we need to be concerned about in our relationship with others is that we recognize their liberty to arrive at their own conclusions in applying the principles of the Scriptures to life. We must recognize them as persons. We must not assume an authoritarian role in which we try to impose our own laws upon them. We do have a right to present our case. We do have a right to show our concern. Our approach must be one of compassionate concern and sound reasoning based on Biblical principles. We must also be willing to listen. We can and should derive benefit from others.

Love for Others. Liberty will not be abused as long as it is kept Christian. One of the important principles in keeping it Christian is that it must be guided by love for others. Paul said, "For, brethren, ye have been called unto liberty; only use not liberty for an occasion to the flesh, but by love serve one another" (Galatians 5:13).

The person who is guided by love will never take the attitude "I don't care what others think. I don't see anything wrong with it. I am going to do it anyway."

Paul admonishes us: "But judge this rather, that no man put a stumblingblock or an occasion to fall in his brother's way" (Romans 14:13). "But if thy brother be

111

grieved with thy meat, now walkest thou not charitably. Destroy not him with thy meat, for whom Christ died (Romans 14:15). "It is good neither to eat flesh, not to drink wine, nor any thing whereby thy brother stumbleth, or is offended, or is made weak" (Romans 14:21). "But take heed lest by any means this liberty of yours become a stumblingblock to them that are weak" (1 Corinthians 8:9). Concerning his own path of action, he said, "Wherefore, if meat make my brother to offend, I will eat no flesh while the world standeth, lest I make my brother to offend" (1 Corinthians 8:13).

We are not to conclude that we can never do anything that someone else may not approve. We are, however, to be very concerned that what we do does not bring serious injury to those who may not agree with us. When we let concern for others guide us, there will be some things we will refrain from though we do not have a conviction against them. We will gladly refrain rather than do injury to a brother.

Concern for Testimony and Influence. Jesus taught that we should let our light so shine that we will have a good testimony (Matthew 5:16). Paul said in regard to the use of Christian liberty, "Let not then your good be evil spoken of" (Romans 14:16).

There are two groups we want to influence—sinners and saints. We must not slant our public relations to just one of these groups. In spite of the fact that it may be complex, we must keep the maximum public relations with each group that keeping public relations with both groups will permit. We dare not in our public relations with sinners for evangelistic purposes ride roughshod over the sincere saints whose loyalty to Jesus Christ, the Bible, and the work of God on earth have helped preserve the Church to this hour.

C. CONCLUSION

The Church can stand a degree of difference in matters where there is debate among those who take their Christianity seriously. However, *the Church must be united both in conviction and experience in:* (1) loving God with all the heart, mind, and strength (Matthew 22:37); (2) loving thy neighbor as thyself (Matthew 22:39); (3) a hunger and thirst after righteousness (Matthew 5:6); and (4) peace, harmony, and joy within the Church (Romans 14:16-21).

There can be no valid Christian liberty where these are not observed. Where there is a lack in these areas, we must call for repentance.

If we accept as valid a Christian liberty that does not grow out of these concerns, we throw the Church doors open for anything. Undisciplined liberty becomes the doctrine of the Church. This we cannot allow.

8 | Principles Versus Legalism

Introduction
A. Legalism
   1. The Explanation of Terms
   2. The Fallacy of Ethical Legalism
B. Principles
   1. The Meaning of Principles
   2. The Application of Principles

INTRODUCTION

Both principles and legalism have been mentioned in earlier chapters as they have related to other contexts. However, both need further elaboration.

Legalism is one of the most subtle forces the Christian ever encounters. The conscientious Christian is the one who is most likely to fall prey to the snare of legalism. The conscience becomes entangled with the web of legalism. It binds and depresses its victim. It is an enemy to the very thing it proposes to do. Once the

114

victim desires deliverance, it comes with the greatest difficulty. Surgery upon the conscience is the most painful and most difficult to accept. The victim is afraid that he will become involved with compromise. There is a logic to legalism that is almost impossible to break. It can be broken only when a person admits that it is an unworkable system and recognizes that the New Testament condemns it and sets forth the doctrine of liberty based on principles.

A. LEGALISM

The Explanation of Terms. For clarification, it would be better to speak of two types of legalism: Soteriological legalism (soteriology means *doctrine of salvation)* and ethical legalism. Soteriological legalism is the point of view that bases salvation on works rather than placing it on faith in Christ and His atoning work. Ethical legalism is the kind of legalism that has been previously mentioned in this study. Ethical legalism is the approach to ethics which seeks to express every ethical decision in terms of a law.

Those who either believe in or tend toward soteriological legalism may have a tendency toward ethical legalism. However, it is not necessary to link ethical legalism with soteriological legalism. The person who believes in soteriological legalism is simply saying that righteous works are the basis of his justification. He may or may not believe that righteous obligations are expressed in the framework of ethical legalism.

It is also possible for a person to believe in ethical legalism and not believe in soteriological legalism. A person may be completely convinced that salvation is by grace through faith. This does not tell him whether his ethics will be expressed in the framework of legalism or the framework of principles. The choice of ethical legalism is an incorrect choice, not because it violates grace, but because it fails to recognize the distinction between the New Covenant approach to ethics and the Old Covenant approach.

Soteriological legalism has never been a part of the divine plan. Paul makes that exceedingly clear in Romans 4 and Galatians 3:1-18. Ethical legalism, though not as extreme as Pharisaic legalism, was a part of the divine plan for the people of God under the Old Covenant. In the New Covenant God views His people as being mature. In keeping with this He has delivered us from ethical legalism and has introduced us to Christian liberty.

Some confusion of soteriological legalism and ethical legalism comes from failing to make the distinction between them in Paul's treatment of legalism in Galatians. Paul's first concern in the book is with soteriological legalism. It is the perversion of the gospel of which he speaks in Galatians 1:6-9. The particular form of soteriological legalism that he was combating was linked with the works of Old Covenant law. In Galatians 3:1-18 he refuted the validity of soteriological legalism. He pointed out that such a view was not supported by either the Abrahamic Covenant or the Covenant of Law. He made it clear that the Abrahamic Covenant established the fact that justification is by faith (Galatians 3:6-15). He further made it clear that the Covenant of Law did not and could not introduce soteriological legalism (Galatians 3:15-18).

Paul continues in Galatians to show the folly of going back under Old Covenant law. In addition to the fact that it would not save, it was a step backwards (Galatians 3:19—4:31). It was a backward step because it was trading liberty for ethical legalism. It was exchanging the superior for the inferior. The experience of Old Covenant ethical legalism was that of being under a *paidagogos* or child conductor (Galatians 3:24) and "in bondage under the elements of the world" (Galatians 4:3).

Paul expressed amazement that they would consider exchanging liberty for ethical legalism. He said, "How turn ye again to the weak and beggarly elements, whereunto ye desire again to be in bondage?" (Galatians 4:9).

The Galatians were in danger, not only of soteriological legalism but also of ethical legalism. Paul was pointing out to them that adding ethical legalism to soteriological legalism was compounding their error. This was particularly foolish for one who had experienced both grace and liberty.

The Fallacy of Ethical Legalism. (Ethical legalism is the primary concern of this study when it relates to legalism. From now on, when the word *legalism* is used it will refer to ethical legalism.)

The Pharisees had the most elaborate system of legalism that the world has ever known. It went far beyond the Mosaic Law. *Torah* (Hebrew for law) had become the central principle of Pharisaism. It was as central and as important to Pharisaism as Jesus Christ is to Christianity. The term, *Torah,* is somewhat broader than our word *law.* It refers to the total revelation of God to man. However, the major stress of *Torah* as used by the Pharisees was the same as our word law. We are speaking correctly, therefore, when we say that law was central in Pharisaism.

The principle of law found its manifestation in the oral law or oral tradition. It is called "oral" because it had not been written at the time of Jesus. It was kept alive in the minds of the scribes and rabbis. It was later written down in the Jewish *Talmud.* The *Talmud,* no doubt, is a modification of the Pharisaism of Jesus' day, but it preserves the basic nature of Pharisaism as it existed during Jesus' ministry.

The multiplication of detail in Pharisaism is almost unbelievable. This detail does not come through fully in reading the New Testament. The New Testament only illustrates the error of Pharisaism. Pharisaism sought to explain every detail of life in terms of law. They felt that God was the God of the whole life, and that law was the framework for expressing divine responsibility.

Oral law was necessary because the Mosaic Law did not prescribe a law for every situation of life. Oral law was the product of authoritative bodies of Jewish

118

religious leaders (the Sanhedrin when Jesus was on earth). The scribes propagated what had been settled by the religious authorities. Their teachings are frequently referred to as oral tradition because most of it had come down from the past. In the New Testament it is called the tradition of the elders.

Why was Jesus so opposed to such a means of expressing ethics? The heart of the matter is seen in Jesus' accusation that the Pharisees had "omitted the weightier matters of the law, judgment, mercy, and faith" (Matthew 23:23). It is not that Pharisees had deliberately decided to be unmerciful. They tried to build mercy into their law. The problem is that previously learned law cannot prepare a person for every situation of life. There must be room for freedom to weigh the situation. Love must have room for spontaneity.

Pharisaism could not go against its man-made laws. If these laws did not provide for helping a person in a certain situation, no help could be offered. This is likely what happened in the case of the parable of the Good Samaritan (Luke 10:30-37). The priest and Levite were probably forbidden by oral law to help the man who had fallen prey to thieves. They were not free to help. The Pharisees in time tried to correct the abuses by modifying laws and making new laws, but the individual could not change his path of action until those in authority changed the law.

Jesus accused the Pharisees of "making the word of God of none effect through your tradition, which ye

119

have delivered" (Mark 7:13). The Pharisees were concerned over the fact that Jesus' disciples did not observe the ceremonial washing of hands before eating that was described by their oral law (Mark 7:2-5). Jesus charged that in many ways they violated God's commandments in obeying their own man-made laws (Mark 7:6-13). He gives one illustration of how this was done. In the case of their Corban law, the son was freed from the obligation to *help his father or mother.* The exact nature of what happened is not clear. It appears that the son was referring to being unable to help his parents because he had dedicated what he had to the Temple. This freed him from the obligation of helping his needy parents. It probably not only freed him from obligation, but also forbade him to use what he had dedicated to the Temple to help his parents. Jesus makes it clear that such a law was in basic conflict with God's law.

The legalism of the Pharisees stifled and choked the needed free expression of the heart and the exercise of common sense. Jesus did not suggest an overhaul of legalism, but a rejection of it. They would have probably been willing to have changed and modified certain details in their legalistic system, but they were unwilling to cast the system aside. They were committed to legalism as the proper framework for expressing divine and ethical obligations. Jesus considered such a framework incapable of expressing ethical responsibility. This ruled out any possibility or room for Jesus in Pharisaism. To accept Jesus was to reject the framework of Pharisaic legalism. This was to reject Pharisaism.

(The above observations on Pharisaism are based on a study made by the author in preparing the thesis, *A Study of Jesus' Encounter With The Pharisees* in partial fulfilment of the requirements for the degree of Master of Theology for the Chicago Graduate School of Theology, 1970. Anyone interested in being introduced to the minute detail of Pharisaic legalism should read *The Babylonian Talmud* in *Selection* translated and edited by Leo Auerbach, New York: Philosophical Library, c. 1944.)

There is no danger that anyone will produce a system of legalism as detailed as that of the Pharisees. However, the basic tendencies of legalism plague many. There are two ways legalism expresses itself. (1) The only ethical responsibility of the Christian is expressed in the laws of the New Testament. Outside these laws license is permitted and practiced. This produces a morally anemic experience. It is a gross misunderstanding of New Testament liberty. It fails to see the stewardship responsibility of the New Covenant believer to apply the principles of the New Testament to life situations. It is akin, in principle, to the legalism of the Sadducees. They recognized no moral authority beyond the most literal interpretation of the first five books of the Old Testament. They recognized no extension of principles to situations not covered in these books.

(2) All ethical responsibility takes the form of law. This includes laws stated in the New Testament. In

addition, it is the believer's responsibility to take the principles of the New Testament and translate them into laws for life situations.

Let us elaborate more fully upon the second type of legalism mentioned above. All ethical decisions are a matter of conscience. Everything is either right or wrong. Acts of love are not free expressions, but obligations. This destroys the basic nature of love. The heart asks: "How may I show my love? Is there something I can do that will help or improve things?" The conscience asks: "What is my obligation?" When every act of love is a matter of conscience, one can never feel a sense of pleasure by going beyond the call of duty.

It is obvious that such an approach to ethics contributes to the development of a highly introspective personality. The person is forever looking to see if there is some detail he has overlooked. He is in bondage. He oscillates between feelings of inferiority and superiority. For the most part, he is overwhelmed by the feeling of inferiority. He is afraid he has not detected every obligation. His list of laws may not be complete. He has hang-ups and exaggerated feelings of guilt. Occasionally, the shift changes and he experiences the feeling of superiority. He is sure that God is proud of anyone who is so sincere about right and wrong. Certainly, he must be a good Christian to be taking matters so seriously. Surely there is going to be some great breakthrough of God's blessing in his life, he thinks.

One of the greatest fallacies of legalism is that it

makes a person self-centered. The experience of introspection described above is the description of a self-centered person. Christian ethics must be Christ-centered. The legalist, in his search to please Jesus, actually defeats his purpose. He takes his eyes off the very one he is supposed to follow, love, admire, and worship.

Legalism tends to produce mechanical obedience. Outward conformity can be done without the person having his heart in it. Insincere conformity may be taken for obedience. Another form of mechanical obedience is found in those who are most sincere. They are so sincere they hurt. Such a heavy reliance upon law has stifled true heart motivation. They have crushed their ability to have normal feelings of the heart.

Legalism at times gets caught in its own snare and makes a person take a path of action his better judgment tells him not to take. This may well be the case of the son who was not allowed by Corban law to help his parents (Mark 7:10-13). This could have also been the case of the priest and Levite who did not help the man who had fallen prey to thieves (Luke 10:30-37).

Many people are caught up in the net of legalism about asking the blessing over food. The problem comes in trying to decide when to ask the blessing other than at meal time. For people of a legalistic turn of mind who eat a lot of between-meal-snacks, this can be a real problem. Their conscience tells them to ask the blessing over every snack. If we are to ask the blessing over food, they can figure no logical reason not to ask it over a snack. Their common sense tells them it is unreasonable to ask the blessing over every snack. They either obey their conscience and feel stupid, or they obey their common sense and feel guilty. I am not suggesting that people should disobey their consciences, but I am suggesting that something needs to be done to correct a misguided conscience.

Another fallacy of legalism is that it creates the possibility through mental gymnastics of a person justifying a deed that is obviously wrong. It is apparently this abuse of legalism that Jesus had in mind when He made the accusation against the Pharisees, "Ye devour widows' houses" (Matthew 23:14). The inadequacy of legalism is seen in our judicial system. Cases are thrown out of court over technical points when the person has admitted guilt. Judges are at times required by law to render decisions that are opposed to their own common sense. We dare not equate that which is legal in the courts with the moral. They may for the most part be the same, but sometimes legal responsibility and moral responsibility are not the same. What about the person who declares bankruptcy and settles with his creditors for less than what he owes them and feels no obligation to make it up later?

Legalism is one of the most deceptive tools ever designed by the devil. It fails to accomplish its intended goal. It is inadequate and fallacious as an expression of ethics. It binds and enslaves its victim. It takes his eyes off Christ. It takes the joy out of his Christian experience. People may admire him, but they do not want to be like him.

B. PRINCIPLES

The Meaning of Principles. When we talk about principles versus laws, we are not suggesting that there are no laws in the New Testament. We are saying that ethical responsibility is not fully expressed in laws, and it should not be. Principles are basic truths that can be applied to a situation. It is not necessary to refer to a list of situations to which it can be applied. The person makes a decision simply on the basis that the application of the principle seems to be appropriate in the situation.

The laws stated in the New Testament not only have literal application, they are also useful as a source of drawing principles for life situations where the literal situations may not exist. For example, "Thou shalt not commit adultery" may in its literal statement refer only to the act of adultery. From this law can be derived the principle that we should avoid that which leads to, desires, or condones adultery. It is the application of the principle that Jesus is speaking of when He said, "Whosoever looketh on a woman to lust after her hath committed adultery with her already in his heart" (Matthew 5:28).

We can also draw principles from teachings that may not take the form of law. For example, Paul spoke against those who "not only do the same [the things mentioned in verses 29-31], but have pleasure in them that do them" (Romans 1:32). The words "have pleasure" are translated from the same word in the Greek that is translated "consenting" in Acts 8:1 where it reads, "And Saul was consenting unto his death." The meaning is that Saul concurred in the stoning of Stephen though he did not cast any stones.

The principle of Romans 1:32 is that it is wrong to concur or delight in seeing others sin. We should not approve or delight in seeing another do something which we would not do ourselves. This is closely akin to Paul's teaching, "Abhor that which is evil; cleave to that which is good" (Romans 12:9).

It is through the application of principles that the Bible remains an up-to-date book. If it were not for the application of principles the Bible would be obsolete. Situations change; principles are permanent. In changing from the legalism of the Old Covenant to the liberty of the New Covenant, God made the New Testament a book that would never need to be updated.

The Application of Principles. The application of principles takes place in the area of the four basic relationships discussed in chapter 4. The principles are amplified from the four basic values in chapter 3.

The four basic values are holiness, love, wisdom, and ideals. Holiness asks the question: Is it right or is it wrong? Love asks the question: How can I show my concern? Wisdom asks the question: What is sound judgment? Ideals ask the question: Is it good or is it bad? (Good in the sense of high value and bad in the

126

sense of low value.)

All of the above questions are important questions for ethics. These questions make it obvious that the concern of ethics goes beyond the concern for right and wrong. Priority is given to righteousness, but it is an immature and shallow Christian experience that does not go beyond this concern for right and wrong. We can never go contrary to right, but some things may clear the test of right that may not be in the best interest of showing concern for others. Paul makes it clear that love constrains us and at times restricts us beyond what righteousness would require (Romans 14 and 1 Corinthians 8). The person who loves God with all his heart and loves his neighbor as himself can never restrict himself to the demands of conscience. He keeps his love in subjection to holiness, but he looks for the full experience that goes beyond the demands of righteousness. He would not dare hurt a Christian brother by doing something he thought was permissible if it would bring injury to his fellow Christian. He would not dare engage in that which passed his own conscience if it would hinder him in winning sinners to Christ.

New Covenant liberty is also concerned with wisdom. One of the requirements of the first deacons was wisdom (Acts 6:3). There is the wisdom of the world that is not subjected to the discipline of Christian values. The wisdom of the Christian must be subjected to the discipline of Christian values. Good judgment does not have the force of law. It cannot be totally ignored, but it does allow room for negotiation in group

127

situations. We respect the opinions of others. When we equate our judgment with right, we give it an unbending nature. This makes group harmony impossible if others do not submit to us.

Ideals may not be as high on the priority list as other values, but they are essential. We cannot ignore ideals. Ideals with the emphasis on good give a stress to quality in life. Ideals have an uplifting influence. It is not our prerogative to set them aside (Philippians 4:8).

In the exercise of Christian liberty, we ask the questions raised by the basic values. We keep our minds alert for principles in the New Testament. We come to life's situations, not with a law book, but with a set of principles that have been embedded in our hearts and minds. The task is not so burdensome that we turn toward introspection. We are free. We can be Christ-centered, not self-centered. We are free to love others. We can enjoy the beauty and blessings of God's creation.

9 | Realistic Idealism Versus Perfectionism

Introduction
A. Perfectionism
   1. Types of Perfectionism
   2. The Fallacy of Perfectionism
B. The Reasons for Rejecting Perfectionism
   1. The Impractical Nature of Perfectionism
   2. Biblical Basis for Rejecting Perfectionism
C. Realistic Idealism
   1. The Need for Idealism
   2. The Need To Be Realistic

INTRODUCTION

This chapter deals with the practical versus the impractical—the possible versus the impossible. Impossible goals do not serve as real challenges to people. Rather, they become the source of depression, despair, and frustration.

Perfectionism, as we are referring to it, is the goal

129

that places undue stress on the finished, polished job. Nothing less is considered success. The perfectionist cannot accept a situation unless everything is a precise fit and all things fit together in perfect order. This carries over into the whole of life.

Realistic idealism is idealism in that it holds to high ideals. It is realistic in that it faces the reality of the facts of life. It recognizes the fact that absolute success is seldom achieved. It sets its goals within the framework of the possible.

A. PERFECTIONISM

Types of Perfectionism. The first type of perfectionist is well known. He achieves a degree of success in certain areas. For some it may be personal appearance; for others it may be the way they do their work; for others it may be the way they keep their car; for others it may be the way they prepare their assignments, etc.

The second type of perfectionist is not so well known. He either never achieves in any area, or he fails in so many areas that he is never suspected of being a perfectionist. He is a quitter. The very moment he sees that he will not obtain perfection in a particular case he is ready to quit. He has already failed. He sees no use of continuing. He is a perfectionist not by attainment but by goal-setting.

One might ask: How does this tie in with the subject of ethics? The goal of perfection is a moral obligation in the person's mind. The goals that we set for ourselves involve the questions of right and wrong, good and bad.

The Fallacy of Perfectionism. The fallacy is immediately obvious with the second type of perfectionist. He falls prey to the unrealistic demands of perfectionism. He has developed the type of mind that believes that things fall in the category of "all or nothing." He sees no value in relative success. It is either total success or failure. When he sees that he has blown the possibility of total success, he quits. He says, "What's the use?" In his performance, he becomes a shiftless, unstable person. He dreams of success, but it never happens. Within himself he is miserable. He has no self-respect and no self-confidence.

The fallacy is not so obvious in the first type of perfectionist. Since he achieves a degree of success in certain areas, the tendency is to look at his perfectionism as good. However, closer observation will reveal that such a person is actually suffering from his perfectionism.

One of the most obvious fallacies of perfectionism in such a person is seen in the fact that, while it leads to a high degree of success in some areas, there will be other areas completely untouched by the high ideals of his perfectionism. While the perfectionist is taken up with putting a glossy finish on one area of his life, other areas are totally neglected.

The success, in the areas in which it is attained, comes at such a high cost that the person is not able to

131

enjoy the reward of his labor. A strain is placed upon his whole system. Life is an overload. In the course of time, his body and nervous system suffer the consequences of stress from overload.

The perfectionist is often the victim of compulsion. He has already brought his product to an acceptable finish, but he cannot stop. He is driven on to an added finishing touch after his own better judgment tries to tell him it is not necessary. He is a victim who cannot obey his better judgment. This type of perfectionism is illustrated by the student who is well prepared to make an A, but is driven on to several more hours of preparation. He does not see the logic of the extra hours, nor does he feel rewarded for them, but like a person who has a hold on a wire with too much electricity, he cannot turn loose.

Perfectionism calls for precision. It has no room for flexibility. It cannot adapt to a situation. Adaptation and flexibility are signs of compromise, or letting down. It is all or nothing. Everything is either right or wrong. It is unable to make the distinction in values between right and good. What it calls good is equated with right. What it calls bad is wrong. It has no room for the varying importance placed on values in chapters 3 and 4 of this study. All values are a matter of righteousness and have the same degree of inflexibility.

The emphasis on precision and the resultant emphasis on inflexibility lead to dogmatism in positions and arguments. There is no room for "may be" or "could be." Everything is clear-cut. The one who differs is guilty of sin. There can be no respect for the sincerity of the person who differs. He is either sinful or stupid. There is not much room for a distinction between majors and minors. Every error is a major error. Such an approach leads to unnecessary division and strife. People on both sides of a controversy may be the victim of this perfectionist approach. Each is a victim of a misguided conscience. To respect his own conscience means he must doubt the sincerity of the other person.

The emphasis on precision and inflexibility in perfectionism creates a tendency toward legalism (see chapter 8). Legalism seeks to express all ethical obligations in the form of a law. A law is precise. It is inflexible. Thus, it appeals to the perfectionist. The combination of perfectionism and legalism is unbearable to the victim and makes him unbearable to others. He is so sincere he hurts. He wonders why God is not blessing him more. Others may admire him for his sincerity, but they find it hard to fellowship with him. They do not want to be like him.

The perfectionist is frequently a sour, depressed, critical person. He has a negative frame of mind. He sees very little but evil in the world and in the Church. He is a fault finder. He is overly suspicious. A few flaws in a person's life blinds him to all the good that is there. Frequently, he has an uncontrollable urge to correct all the mistakes he sees and hears.

All of the problems discussed above are not found in every perfectionist, but some are. There are some good things that can be said about the perfectionist.

Usually he is a hard worker. Except for the second type described above, he is dependable. He is conscientious. However, the positive points of the perfectionist can be preserved by a more realistic approach without all the liabilities of perfectionism.

B. THE REASONS FOR REJECTING PERFECTIONISM

Perfectionism is difficult to overcome. It is embedded in the conscience. As has been observed earlier in this study, it is not easy to submit to surgery upon the conscience. It is very delicate surgery. The patient fears that he will become guilty of serious compromise.

The Impractical Nature of Perfectionism. The perfectionist is aware that things are not working out as they should. If he has a severe case of perfectionism, he is aware of the fact that he is not happy. It is very difficult for him to admit that his problems are related, to a large extent, to his perfectionism. A study of the fallacy of perfectionism above will aid one in recognizing that his problems are related to his perfectionism. He must desire a more workable goal and be willing to accept an alternative.

Biblical Basis for Rejecting Perfectionism. It is impossible to get away from the concept of a flawless morality. We believe that God is absolutely holy. There is no flaw in Him. As John tells us, "God is light, and in him is no darkness at all" (1 John 1:5). ANY CON-

SCIOUSNESS OF SIN BRINGS THE FEELING OF GUILT. We are to confess our sins and ask for forgiveness (1 John 1:9). We cannot accept sin in our lives. This produces in us a longing for a flawless morality in which all taint of sin is gone. There is a difference between longing for moral perfectionism and setting moral perfectionism for a goal as will be seen in the next paragraph. The ability to recognize this difference can make the difference between misery and defeat on the one hand, and happiness and victory on the other hand.

The longing for moral perfection means that a person does not want to sin. He hates sin in his life. He confesses it and works to overcome it. The goal of moral perfection represents a standard to determine success or failure. When moral perfection is the goal, the failure to reach the goal represents defeat. Defeat brings unhappiness. Unhappiness in life is, to a large extent, related to the gap between what we think we are and what we think we ought to be. The feeling of being forgiven by God contributes to happiness, but happiness also requires a sense of achievement or success. It is difficult for one who has set moral perfection as a goal to have a sense of success.

The question is: Does the Bible give any grounds for accepting anything less than moral perfection as success or victory? I think it does. In 1 John 1:6-7, John contrasts walking in the light and walking in darkness. The one who claims to have fellowship with Jesus Christ and at the same time walks in darkness is a liar (verse 6).

135

Verse 7 speaks about walking in light. Yet, walking in light is not equated with moral perfection. This is evident from the fact that as we walk in light, "the blood of Jesus Christ his Son cleanseth us from all sin." The very fact that there is sin from which one needs cleansing indicates that the person has not achieved moral perfection; yet, he is walking in light. Walking in light certainly represents moral success and victory.

We should long for moral perfection in the sense that we do not accept sin in our lives. At the same time, we must not set moral perfection as a goal by which we determine success or failure. We must set possible goals. We should set as our goal to be basically righteous and to have a good testimony. To be basically righteous is to be in a state in which sin is the exception and righteousness is the rule. To have a good testimony means that sin is controlled to the point that it does not destroy people's confidence in us. Righteousness in our lives builds their confidence.

To be basically righteous and to have a good testimony are possible. Many Christians achieve this goal. A possible goal is a challenge; an impossible goal is depressing. The success of reaching the goal of being basically righteous and having a good testimony contributes to happiness. We have self-respect and self-confidence. We are challenged to do our best.

There are some questions that still need to be answered: (1) What does 1 John 3:9 teach? (2) What is meant by the New Testament teaching on perfection?

First John 3:9 says: "Whosoever is born of God

doth not commit sin." It further adds: "And he cannot sin, because he is born of God." Many have read this verse and have concluded that this verse teaches sinless perfection. This would be a possible interpretation from the English translation, but it is not a possible interpretation from the Greek text.

In the Greek the word for "commit" in "doth not commit sin" is a present indicative verb. In the majority of cases the present tense in the indicative mood indicates the kind of action indicated in the English by the addition of the letters "-ing." The word for "sin" in the Greek in "he cannot sin" is a present infinitive. The present infinitive in Greek *always* refers to the type action indicated by "-ing" in English. Since the present indicative refers to the "-ing" type action in most cases, and the present infinitive does in all cases, we would conclude that the "-ing" type action is the kind referred to in the verse.

Based on the above observations, the following translation would give the correct meaning: "Whosoever is born of God is not committing sin: for his seed remaineth in him: and he cannot be sinning." This does not make it impossible for the Christian to commit an "act" of sin, but it does mean that he cannot practice sin. He cannot be characteristically sinful. Sin will be the exception and not the rule in his life. He will be basically righteous. He is walking in light, not darkness (1 John 1:6, 7).

The above interpretation is true to the Greek text and it harmonizes with other passages which teach that

Christians have to deal with sin in their lives (1 John 1:7—2:1). It should be pointed out that 1 John 3:9 is talking about all Christians, not a select group. It is clearly a reference to all who are born of God.

To reject moral perfection as a goal by which to measure success does not open the way for moral laxness. While 1 John does not teach that we will achieve moral perfection, it insists that the Christian is guided by moral concern. He is one who practices righteousness, not sin.

We have one more hurdle to cross in rejecting perfectionism. What is meant by the New Testament teaching on perfection? In the majority of places in the New Testament where the word *perfect* is found, it is a translation of a Greek word which has as its basic meaning *complete*. This is obvious in 1 Corinthians 13:10. Paul says, "But when that which is perfect is come, then that which is in part shall be done away." In this verse, the "perfect" is contrasted with the "part." It is obvious that the perfect is the whole or the complete.

In most cases the completeness referred to is the completeness that is achieved through growth. Thus, the perfect is the mature. This meaning is obvious in Hebrews 5:14 where the Greek word for perfect is translated by the words "of full age." Paul is telling us that "strong meat belongs to those who through growth and development have reached maturity."

Maturity is obviously the meaning of perfect in Ephesians 4:13. A reading of verses 13 and 14 together shows that the "perfect man" of verse 13 is contrasted

138

with "children" of verse 14. The perfect man has the steadfastness that goes with maturity in contrast to the instability that goes with immaturity.

In 1 Corinthians 14:20 the Greek word for perfect is translated "men." Paul is telling us that in malice we should be like children. We are in understanding to be "perfect," or as the King James Version translates it we are to be "men." We are to be mature in our understanding.

The thrust of completeness seems to be a little different in Matthew 5:48. Jesus said, "Be ye therefore perfect, even as your Father which is in heaven is perfect." Let us read the word *complete* in each of the places where the word *perfect* occurs. This will raise the question: In what way are we to be "complete, even as the Father which is in heaven is complete." In the previous context beginning with verse 43, Jesus had been talking about two kinds of love. One was a love that only loves those who love us. This would be an incomplete love. The other was a love which embraced both those who love us and those who do not. This would be a complete love. The Father showed His love to both the just and the unjust by sending the rain and sunshine to both. This illustrates the complete or perfect love of the Father. We, like the Father, are to have a complete or perfect love that loves both those who love us and those who do not.

In Ephesians 4:12 and 2 Timothy 3:17 Greek words with a different connotation are used. In 2 Timothy 3:17 the meaning of the word *perfect* is

139

explained by the last part of the verse. The perfect man is "throughly [thoroughly] furnished unto all good works." He is a prepared person. He is equipped for service.

In Ephesians 4:12 Paul speaks of "perfecting the saints." The Greek word for *perfecting* is closely related to the word for *perfect* in 2 Timothy 3:17. The meaning is "the equipping of the saints for the work of the ministry."

The idea of flawlessness is not the meaning of the Greek word for perfect. The reference in most places is to the complete in contrast with the incomplete, or the finished with the unfinished. An unfinished building would not be perfect even if the workmanship were not flawless. The person who is mature physically is perfect even though he is not flawless. The child would not be perfect even if he were flawless in his physical body. It is also obvious that when perfect refers to "equipping," flawlessness is not the point of emphasis.

When we are challenged to be perfect in the New Testament, we are challenged to be mature, complete, and equipped. Certainly, this would call for moral concern and progress, but it does not entangle us with the depressing goal of moral perfection.

C. REALISTIC IDEALISM

It is not enough to reject perfectionism. We must construct a workable alternative that will preserve the good that goes with perfectionism without the liabilities that go with perfectionism.

The Need for Idealism. The rejection of perfectionism must not be followed by a rejection of ideals. The Scripture challenges us to high standards and high ideals. To think about Christianity and not think about high standards and high ideals is to grossly misunderstand Christianity. Lack of concern in matters relating to holiness, love, wisdom, and ideals makes the whole system of Christian life and thought suffer.

Though much internal difficulty is created by the unrealistic demands of perfectionism, our being will not accept the position of unconcern as a way out. To give value to the right and good and to give disvalue to the wrong and the bad are written so indelibly in the human heart and mind that they cannot be erased. We can never accept a goal that does not represent a good effort on our part.

If our experience measures up to what we recognize as good, we will build our self-esteem. If our experience fails to measure up to or approximate what we recognize as good, our self-esteem will suffer accordingly. These are facts that we cannot change about ourselves. In our conscious minds we may try to argue against these facts, but we cannot escape the judgment of our deep inner self. We may be able to weaken the sense of conscious guilt, but we cannot escape the judgment of our inner self, as it is manifested in a lowering of our self-esteem when we fail to perform the right and the good.

In order to avoid the consequences of the wrong and the bad we may practice "label-changing." We know that we place value on the right and the good and disvalue on the wrong and the bad. If we want to engage in the wrong and the bad, we seek to place the labels of right and good on the matters under consideration. We may be able to fool ourselves on the conscious level, but our deep inner self is not fooled. It knows what our true interest is.

The only way to build self-esteem and self-respect is to follow the path of truth, right, and good. It is not simply a matter of being acceptable to God. It is a matter of being acceptable to ourselves. If we follow the path of label-changing, we will suffer the consequences. Our basic nature of giving value to the right and the good and disvalue to the wrong and the bad cannot be changed. Our only hope of happiness is to recognize this fact and live accordingly. When sin is the exception and not the rule in our lives, we can experience the needed relief by forgiveness; but we can accept ourselves only when we are basically righteous and have a reasonable degree of success with the good.

The Need To Be Realistic. The Bible clearly teaches that we should be happy in this life (Matthew 11:28-30; John 14:27; 15:11; Galatians 5:22; Romans 14:17; and 1 John 1:3-4). Note that the Greek word translated "blessed" in the beatitudes (Matthew 5:3-12) is the word for happy. When we take these teachings along with the fact that we will not achieve moral perfection nor the highest standard of excellence in all of our endeavors, it is obvious that God wants us to be happy with something less than perfection. We must be realistic in our goal-setting. Our goals must be within the framework of the possible. They must take into account our frailties as well as our strengths. On the one hand our goals must be low enough that we can either reach them or get reasonably close. On the other hand, they must be high enough that we can respect them.

Realistic goals are a challenge because they are possible. They actually bring a higher degree of achievement in excellence than perfectionist goals. Perfectionist goals are depressing and discouraging. They produce a drag on life. Realistic goals produce confidence, challenge, and happiness. The perfectionist may excel in a few areas, but other areas will suffer. Realistic goals give a better opportunity for a more even spread of excellence in life.

Our own lack of ability in certain areas and the demand of other considerations make the highest degree of excellence impossible at times. The realistic approach makes it possible for one to weigh his abilities, to examine the priorities of life, and to accept as success what is reasonably possible under the circumstances. The perfectionist is incapable of such reasoning. He is caught in the web of a false sense of guilt. False guilt is harder to cope with than real guilt. Real guilt demands a *possible* change. False guilt demands an *impossible* change. The sense of guilt deepens because the perfectionist is sure that true repentance will bring a change, but he is caught in a situation where the required change

143

is impossible.

The realistic approach avoids the negativism that goes with perfectionism. The perfectionist is hung up on unconquered territory. The realistic approach enables one to take an honest look at unconquered territory, but at the same time allows him to count the success of conquered territory. Perfectionism demands the highest degree of success now. Realistic idealism recognizes the place of growth in reaching the highest standard of excellence.

The realistic approach cannot be used to set aside our desire to achieve excellence. Realistic idealism recognizes the place of ideals. It insists that we should not have so many irons in the fire that we spread ourselves so thin that satisfactory excellence cannot be maintained. Regardless of what emphasis we give in our conscious minds to quantity, our deep inner self will never let us neglect quality without suffering the consequences. Realistic idealism meets man's need of high ideals and his need to set goals that make success possible.

10 When Values Conflict

Introduction
A. The Importance of Distinguishing Values from Each Other
    1. The Problem of Flexibility and Inflexibility
    2. The Problem Priority
B. When Holiness and Love Conflict
    1. Holiness and Love in God
    2. The Area of Conflict Between Holiness and Love
    3. Holiness and Love in Maintaining Law and Order
    4. Holiness and Love in Maintaining Discipline
    5. Holiness and Love in Standing for Right
    6. Holiness and Love in War
C. Wisdom in the Order of Priorities
    1. The Subjection of Wisdom to Holiness
    2. The Flexibility of Wisdom
    3. Wisdom and Love
D. Ideals in the Order of Priorities
    1. The Subjection of Ideals to Holiness
    2. The Flexibility of Ideals
E. When Any Alternative Seems To Be Wrong

INTRODUCTION

The four basic values are holiness, love, wisdom, and ideals. The relative value of these was discussed in chapter 3. In this chapter the significance of recognizing the relative value of these values to each other will be discussed. In real life situations, all values cannot reach the highest degree of fulfilment in every case. What path of action do we follow in such cases?

A. THE IMPORTANCE OF DISTINGUISHING THE VALUES FROM EACH OTHER

The Problem of Flexibility and Inflexibility. The matter of flexibility and inflexibility is closely related to the relative and the absolute. The relative is flexible and the absolute is inflexible.

Life must have both the absolute and the relative. The unchanging nature of absolutes gives stability and assurance. The possibility of change that goes with relative truth gives the needed freedom for adaptation and progress.

If we should try to make everything relative, there can be no unifying factors. There can be no standards. Every man becomes a law unto himself. Some who propose to take such a position are inconsistent. They use the denials of absolutes to undermine the absolutes held by others while imposing their own thoughts upon people. They are seeking to establish a new system of absolutes while claiming to reject all absolutes.

If we should try to make everything absolute and not subject to change, we stifle initiative and in the long run we make unity impossible. If everything is absolute there can be no room for the creative mind. Under such circumstances, unity is possible only as one mind imposes itself upon others. When this ceases to work, there is no room for a compromise settlement regardless of what the issue may be. Everything is either right or wrong.

Only holiness raises the question: Is it right or is it wrong in the moral sense? Love, wisdom, and ideals deal with right and wrong only as they occupy a common ground with holiness. Love, wisdom, and ideals deal with good and bad when they do not occupy a common ground with holiness. (See chapter 3.)

When right and wrong are involved, there is no flexibility. When good and bad are involved, there is room for flexibility. If one equates or confuses the values of love, wisdom, and ideals with holiness, a serious problem develops. Wherever he sees value, he sees right and wrong. All values are inflexible. A negotiated settlement would bring compromise. The only way to reach a working agreement is for the other party to recant. Division is a price that can be paid over any issue.

On the other hand, if the flexibility of love, wisdom, and ideals is read into holiness, tragic results follow. All corners can be rounded. Every conviction and every doctrine will ultimately run the risk of

147

surgery from the knife of compromise. There can be no effective dealing with ethical issues until we find the proper place for flexibility and inflexibility. This means that we must know the particular value with which we are dealing. Is it holiness, love, wisdom, or ideals?

The Problem of Priority. Since holiness is inflexible, it always has top priority in values. However, the question is not so simple when it comes to love, wisdom, and ideals. As a rule the greatest flexibility is found with ideals. There is no simple solution in settling the problem of priority. The beginning point is the recognition of the fact that there are times when all values will not be suggesting the same path of action. In such cases, if holiness is not involved, the situation will have to be weighed. The person, under such circumstances, should take the path of action that seems to him to have priority. Such decisions should be sincerely dealt with, but the person should not be guided by fear. Lack of concern in such areas might infer moral guilt, but moral guilt is not involved simply on the grounds that the best path of action is not taken. (See 1 Corinthians 7:36-38.)

B. WHEN HOLINESS AND LOVE CONFLICT

Holiness and Love in God. We tend to shy away from the idea that there is conflict in God. Yet it seems that we cannot understand the functioning of God's holiness and love without concept of conflict. By

148

conflict we do not mean to suggest that there is or was a battle between holiness and love. We mean that holiness and love do not always suggest the same path of action. There is no battle because love always bows willingly to the demand of holiness.

Holiness demanded that the sins of man be punished. Love desired to save man. It was the work of divine wisdom that devised a plan whereby both holiness and love could be satisfied. Holiness stood inflexibly by its demands that sin be punished. Love sent Jesus Christ to submit to that punishment for the human race.

There is no greater example to be found anywhere of the inflexibility of holiness than at the cross of Christ. The inflexibility of holiness would not allow even the Son of God to save us from our sins without first paying for them.

The flexibility of love and inflexibility of holiness is seen at the final judgment. Those who fail to receive Jesus Christ in this life must submit to the inflexible demands of holiness and be cast into hell for eternity (Revelation 20:11-15 and 21:8). The greatest love in the universe will submit to the holiness of God. That love satisfied holiness and provided redemption for all who will come to Jesus Christ, but it will not seek to stay the hand of God's wrath from those who refuse Jesus Christ.

The Area of Conflict Between Holiness and Love. There is an area of common ground between love and holiness. Paul lists the commandments that deal with our relationship to others. Then he said, "Love is the fulfilling of the law" (Romans 13:9-10). Love has the same interest that holiness has when it comes to treating people right in our everyday relationships. Love shares this common ground because "Love worketh no ill to his neighbor" (verse 10). Love avoids that which brings hurt to another.

Holiness and love do not share a common ground when the path required by holiness "hurts" another. Holiness does not hurt for the sake of hurting. It avoids hurting where possible, but in human experience it is not always possible to avoid hurting people while at the same time standing for right. Justice in judicial proceedings is the work of holiness, not love. Every strong stand and defense of right is the work of holiness, not love.

Holiness and Love in Maintaining Law and Order. Justice issues from holiness. Arrests, prosecution, conviction, and punishment of those who violate the law depends upon justice, not love. Punishment hurts. Love does not bring hurt to people. The penal system works on the assumption that the law violator is guilty and deserves to be punished.

While there is a clear distinction between justice and love, justice should not be divorced from love. Justice needs to be tempered by love. Justice needs a heart. Without a heart it becomes a cold and unmerciful tyrant who with a spirit of vengeance gleefully punishes its victim. When it does, it ceases to be justice. Justice moves out of obligation, not out of the spirit of

150

vengeance. The strong arm of justice is to be exercised with a heavy heart. Justice and love need each other. To subtract one destroys the other.

It is the combination of justice and love that makes the treatment of criminals both penal and rehabilitative. The penal aspect comes from justice. The rehabilitative aspect comes from love.

Holiness and Love in Maintaining Discipline. The statement is frequently made, "I whip my child because I love him." I think this is a wrong analysis of the case. The logic of love may motivate one to whip a child, but not the emotion of love. A parent may reason that it is in the best interest of the child to discipline him, but he does not have a deep feeling of love when he carries out the responsibility. Discipline draws from the firm side of our nature, not the tender side. Jesus was well known for his compassion, but when He ran the moneychangers out of the Temple no one would have said, "My, how He loves. What compassion!" That occasion drew on the firm side of Jesus' nature, not the tender side.

In discipline holiness must be tempered by love, and love must be tempered by holiness. If love is not tempered by holiness, it becomes spineless sentimentality. It does not want to hurt. In such cases, the absence of reasoned-firmness means that discipline occurs only when the parent is provoked to a state of uncontrolled anger. The child never knows what to expect.

When holiness is not tempered by love, it becomes firm, rigid, and heartless. Guilt is attached to every form of misbehavior. There is no room for anything to be explained as a misunderstanding or as an accident. Whipping or some other form of punishment is the only way to bring correction.

The tragedy is that both holiness and love cease to exist when they cease to exist in combination. Holiness gives the touch of firmness that is needed. Love gives the touch of tenderness that is needed. Wisdom discovers the proper combination of firmness and tenderness.

Holiness and Love in Standing for Right. Holiness recognizes the need for taking a stand on basic issues. It recognizes the fact that Christianity cannot exist apart from basic truth and morality. It calls for firmness, courage, and forthrightness.

Love recognizes the need for giving due consideration to the other person. When possible, it grants sincerity to the other person. It seeks to win the other person rather than to subdue him if that approach is at all possible. It seeks to avoid all unnecessary division.

If holiness is not tempered by love, it becomes contaminated and will eventually cease to be holiness. It imputes moral guilt to the opponent wherever there is a difference. Differences cannot be considered a misunderstanding. The other party must recognize his guilt and repent. The person who is guided by such an attitude is quick to pay the price of division. He rides roughshod over the feelings and thoughts of others who get in his way.

If love is not tempered by holiness, the fundamentals of the faith and the morality of the Ten Commandments will eventually be compromised. Nothing can be said that would hurt anybody. Division is worse than heresy. A negotiated settlement can be reached on any issue.

The basic priority of holiness must be preserved, but holiness must be accompanied by love. To subordinate holiness to love is to eventually destroy or seriously weaken holiness.

The wise defender of theological and moral issues will seek to be known as both a man of courage and a man of compassion. A man who combines both courageous firmness and compassion may not readily be understood. When he is firm, people may wonder if he can be compassionate. When he is compassionate, people may wonder if he can be firm. It is only when people have learned the true roles of holiness and love that they will be able to understand the person who combines both of these values in his experiences.

The beginning point in understanding those who properly combine holiness and love in their experience is to understand God. The same God who loved us so much He sent Jesus to die for us will punish in hell those who do not receive Jesus Christ as Lord and Savior. The same Jesus who wept at the grave of Lazarus ran the moneychangers out of the Temple. The same Jesus who ate with sinners that He might win them sternly rebuked the Pharisees.

Holiness and Love in War. In describing an ideal society, no one would have a place for war in that society. There would be no disputes that could not be settled by negotiation. If the utopian picture is taken far enough, there would be no disputes to settle. All values could be upheld and fulfilled without hurt to anybody. The problem is that we do not live in that kind of society.

The Christian shrinks back from the idea of killing. He abhors the idea of inflicting injury upon people and bringing destruction upon their land. It is only when he can see a worse situation developing that he can resort to warfare.

War is the most *horrible* experience this side of hell, but it is not the *worst* experience. The worst experience is to be denied the right to be a free human being, and the right to fulfil one's responsibility to God as he understands it. When war for this freedom is the only alternative to the loss of this freedom, right must prevail though love is denied expression. No country can be expected to allow itself to be overrun by another country without offering to defend itself. To deny a country the right to protect itself by resorting to war is the same as denying an individual the right to kill in self-defense.

Though a Christian may participate in war with a clear conscience, he does so with a heavy heart. He is saddened by the fact that circumstances have arisen which made it impossible to avoid war. He must avoid bitterness and hatred. Love is severely limited and finds few outlets in war, but it must temper to whatever extent is possible the conduct of the Christian in war.

C. WISDOM IN THE ORDER OF PRIORITIES

The Subjection of Wisdom to Holiness. The Bible speaks about two kinds of wisdom—wisdom that is earthly and wisdom that is from above (James 3:15-18). The earthly wisdom is called sensual and devilish and is associated with envying, strife, confusion, and every evil work (James 3:15-16). The wisdom from above is pure, peaceable, gentle, easy to be intreated, full of mercy and good fruits, without partiality, and without hypocrisy. It is associated with righteousness (James 3:17-18).

By Biblical standards, earthly wisdom is not wisdom. As Paul says, "Hath not God made foolish the wisdom of this world?" (1 Corinthians 1:20). It is called wisdom by the world because it seems to bring success in terms of material gain, or get one off the hook in time of trouble. A lie about a product may bring in a higher price. Underhanded dealing may help one pull a fast deal. Such wisdom is called foolishness by God because it does not recognize the divine value system. The temporary gains of such wisdom are followed by long-term ruin.

The wisdom from above recognizes the divine value system. Wisdom recognizes the value of love and ideals, but it also recognizes the fact that they have flexibility. When it comes to holiness, wisdom submits to its inflexibility. Judgment can never be called good judgment that requires one to violate morality or the clear teachings of the Scriptures. It is on the recognition of the subjection of wisdom to holiness that the statement is based which says: "It is never right to do wrong to do right."

Holiness insists that the statement, "The end justifies the means," is wrong. Plans to reach good goals must be subject to holiness. It is better to fail than to use unrighteous means to reach good goals. Plans to promote the gospel must not violate the clear teaching of the Scriptures. The statement of Paul, "I am made all things to all men, that I might by all means save some" (1 Corinthians 9:22), is grossly misunderstood if one does not recognize that the "means" must pass the test of holiness and the Scriptures.

The Flexibility of Wisdom. It is important that we distinguish between holiness and wisdom. Whenever a person equates what he considers good judgment with righteousness, he places the same value on wisdom that he does on holiness. This gives inflexibility to wisdom. The person with this viewpoint fights as fiercely for a point of judgment as he does for holiness.

The leader who equates his judgment with righteousness either runs a one-man show, or he is brought to defeat. If he is powerful enough, he crushes those who get in his way. He has no room for a negotiated settlement. That would be compromise.

It is important to see that all compromise is not sinful. We cannot compromise holiness because it is inflexible. Wisdom is flexible. When a conflict exists over what is considered wisdom, there is no sin committed when a workable solution is developed that will preserve as much as possible of the interest of each group. Yet, such a solution involves compromise.

One might ask: "Does not holiness require that a solution be reached that will preserve the unity of a body if it can be done within reason?" Is not the obligation to Paul's admonition, "If it be possible, as much as lieth in you, live peaceably with all men" (Romans 12:18), a righteous obligation? There can be no peace, fellowship, or unity in a group situation if there are not some things that can be settled by a negotiated settlement. The majority rule in a democratic organization should not turn into a battle between forces to see which side can defeat the other.

I am not saying that a person should not promote what he considers good judgment. But I am saying that he should respect the Christian sincerity and the rights of others. He should keep in mind the value of unity. He should be sure that he does not create a worse problem by his approach than the problem he is solving. He should recognize the flexibility of wisdom.

Wisdom and Love. Love is not subject to wisdom in the same sense that it is to holiness. Love needs the guidance of wisdom. Love wants to help and help now. Wisdom give the realistic touch to love.

There are some problems that have no quick solution. For example, the problem of poverty. Love, without the guidance of wisdom, would be ready to empty its pockets to the poor. This would not solve the problem of poverty. Happiness requires more than material goods. It requires self-respect. A person can respect himself only if he is earning his own living, when

157

it is possible. Handouts work against helping people develop self-respect. Wisdom allows love the privilege of giving to those in need, but it insists that it be done in such a way that it helps a person develop self-respect. It seeks to make them responsible, productive citizens.

Another problem that has no quick solution is the racial problem. Wisdom recognizes that there are no overnight solutions. It insists that means must not be used that build barriers between the races. Wisdom builds slowly, but surely. It seeks to make progress by building mutual respect. It seeks to move as rapidly as the realities of the case will permit.

D. IDEALS IN THE ORDER OF PRIORITIES

The Subjection of Ideals to Holiness. The nature of ideals must be compatible with high morals. This means the rejection of any form of art that promotes or condones immodesty and immorality. We dare not allow art, music, or literature to escape the sanctifying influence of holiness.

In the broader context ideals promote the high, the lofty, and the noble. Ideals promote refinement and excellence. The pursuit of ideals must always be subjected to holiness. For example, in our pursuit of the better things of life we must live within our income. We must settle for a lower quality before we would fail to pay our debts.

The Flexibility of Ideals. It is important that we not equate good taste with holiness. On the other hand holiness does have an interest in ideals. Holiness will not tolerate the repudiation of ideals. Holiness cannot ignore sloppiness. However, where there is an interest in ideals, holiness does not seek to spell out the details. There is more freedom in the matter of ideals than in either love or wisdom. There must be room for differences in taste. Not all people like the same color combinations. Not all people like the same pattern. While we should permit variations in the area of ideals, we cannot tolerate a total rejection of the category of ideals.

E. WHEN ANY ALTERNATIVE SEEMS TO BE WRONG

This problem is not so great when it is a matter of wisdom or ideals. What is difficult is when it seems that either approach seems to be wrong. For example, working on the assumption that abortion is wrong because it is taking the life of an unborn child, what about performing an abortion to save the life of the mother? It seems that both to fail to save the life of the mother and to take the life of the unborn child are wrong. Yet, one of these must be done. Most would save the mother's life.

In such cases there is no easy answer. No foolproof arguments can be produced. What a person has to do is to decide what he can best live with. Trust the

159

matter into the hands of God and move forward with the responsibilities of life. When, with our whole heart, we want to do the right thing, we must not become burdened down with guilt over the choice we make.

11 | Personal Development and Personal Relationships

Introduction
A. Personal Development
   1. Character Development
   2. Personality Development
   3. Development of Proper Role as Men and Women
B. Basic Personal Relationships
   1. Our Relationship with Our Neighbor
   2. Our Relationship with Other Christians
   3. Our Relationship with Our Enemies
   4. Biblical Admonitions with Regard to Our One-Another Relationships

INTRODUCTION

By personal development we mean the development of our own personality. The concern in this study is with the involvement of ethics in that development.

By personal relationships we mean the relationships that we have with others. The concern here is the influence of ethics upon these relationships.

A. PERSONAL DEVELOPMENT

Character Development. The Christian has no other responsibility in life that is equal to that of being the right kind of person. Being the right kind of person is more important than performing service for God. This is not to suggest that there is a conflict between being the right kind of person and serving. A person should do both. Service needs to be performed by holy people. Untold damage is done when weakness of character is found in the lives of those who occupy leadership positions in the church.

It is imperative that the church strengthen its emphasis on character development. If we go back a few decades, we go back to a culture that accepted Christian values for its ideals. Christianity furnished the conscience for society. This did not mean that everybody lived by these ideals, but it does mean that by general consensus of opinion Christian ideals were considered right. Strong character was emphasized in school and in society. In most places there was no controversy over basic Christian values.

Today, we live in a secular society. The Bible is no longer considered the "Good Book" by everybody. Getting ahead in life, making more money, and having a good time receive greater stress than the necessity of using the right means to achieve those goals. Society is not doing for our youth what it once did in the matter of values. To a large extent it is an opponent of the Christian system of values.

It takes far more effort to instill values in a day when society is to a large extent an opponent of Christian values than it did when society was a friend of Christian values. Such values as honesty, duty, and moral purity must receive constant stress in all phases of our church programs.

Paul gave a strong emphasis to honesty. In Romans 12:17 he says, "Provide things honest in the sight of all men." The meaning of the Greek word for provide is to "think before." It calls for advance planning. The verse also calls for an interest in appearing to be honest in the sight of all men. It is not enough to be honest. We must deliberately plan to appear to others to be honest. In 2 Corinthians 8:16-21, Paul manifests this concern with reference to the offering for the saints at Jerusalem. The churches chose a man of high reputation to go along with Paul to avoid any blame being cast upon Paul for the way he handled the offering (verses 18-20). This Paul called, "Providing for honest things, not only in the sight of the Lord, but also in the sight of men" (verse 21).

The honest man always seeks the truth and speaks the truth. He weighs the evidence of a damaging message before he believes it. He not only avoids outright lying, but also avoids speaking the truth in such a way that he intentionally leaves false impressions. He does not take credit that belongs to others. He gives credit to whom credit is due. He pays his bills and pays them on time. If he cannot pay on time, he explains his problem to the person he owes and seeks to take care of the matter in the most satisfactory way possible. He respects the property rights of others (Exodus 20:15).

A person of noble character has a strong sense of duty. He is responsible, dependable, and reliable. He is prompt. He does not waste another person's time by keeping him waiting unless unavoidable circumstances arise. He gives a day's work for a day's pay. He gives a day's pay for a day's work (Jeremiah 22:13). He gives honor and respect to whom such is due (Exodus 20:12 and Romans 13:7). He gives proper respect to government (Romans 13:1-7). In pursuing his duties in life, he looks for ways to keep going, not ways to stop. He is not lazy. He may suffer from fatigue at times but he is building the reward of self-respect.

The person of character is deeply concerned about moral purity. The concern for "Thou shalt not commit adultery" (Exodus 20:14) goes beyond the letter of the law. Interest in purity takes precedence over styles. The young lady who is deeply interested in purity will dress modestly, even at the cost of popularity. The young man who desires to be pure labors to be victorious over lustful thoughts (Matthew 5:27-28). Those who want to be pure do not carelessly engage in bodily contact in courtship (1 Corinthians 6:18). Only those who hunger and thirst after righteousness will be able to develop and live by sound convictions in matters of purity. We cannot sell high standards in matters of sex to those who do not hunger and thirst after righteousness.

Personality Development. Our personality is the way we think, feel, and act. Character is involved in this, but it was felt that it was better to give separate treatment to character. Our concern with personality is with the practical functions of life.

There is a degree of fixity in personality that comes as we grow older, but there is also room for change. The person who is shy, timid, and overly reserved does not have to remain that way. The self-centered person who is taken up with over-introspection can do something about it. The person who is bitter and sour can change. A person does not have to continue in self-pity, depression, and despair.

It is not only possible to improve our personality, but also our obligation. God expects us to have a good testimony (Matthew 5:16). Part of having a good testimony is to experience joy, peace, satisfaction, and contentment. The spiritually mature person demonstrates these experiences.

I am not saying that a person can change overnight. Personality change requires the process of growth. Growth brings about in one's life the experience of the fruit of the Holy Spirit which is: "Love, joy, peace, longsuffering, gentleness, goodness, faith, meekness, temperance [self-discipline]" (Galatians 5:22-23). Added to this list is what Paul says in Ephesians 5:9, "For the fruit of the Spirit is in all goodness and righteousness and truth." Note the contrast in the experiences involved in the fruit of the Spirit with the personality traits described in the second paragraph above. The personality traits listed as the fruit of the Spirit *can* and *should* be ours.

The matter of personality change involves the whole process of spiritual growth. Our present study does not call for a full elaboration of the process of spiritual growth as it relates to personality development. The following will prove to be helpful.

1. Develop an outgoing personality.
   a. Put God in the center of your life. Turn your thoughts toward Him.
   b. Love other people. Work on being friendly. Work on being accommodating.
   c. Be observant. Notice the things around about you. Make this a regular practice.
2. Develop a good self-image.
   a. Recognize the value of your strong points. Do not become hung up on your weakness.
   b. Recognize the value of your successes. Do not become hung up on your failures.
   c. Recognize your blessings. Do not become hung up on your problems.
   d. Develop self-confidence by setting and reaching short-term goals.
   e. Avoid idealistic goals. Set realistic goals that can be reached, or at least approximated.
   f. Do right so you can respect yourself for moral integrity.

g. Forgive yourself of your mistakes.

Our personality has been programmed by certain ideas, attitudes, and dispositions. We have been conditioned a certain way. A change of personality comes by reprogramming ourselves with new ideas, attitudes, and dispositions. By continued practice of the things listed above we can program our personality in the direction of being more outgoing and toward having a better self-image.

Development of Proper Role as Men and Women. While men and women have much in common, the Bible recognizes that there are some differences in the roles of men and women. This fact has always been recognized by Biblical Christianity. The Bible gives no precise, clear-cut description of what the differences are. Christians are not in complete agreement on what these differences are. It is my purpose to make a few basic observations. It is not my purpose to fully elaborate the subject.

It is important that a young man develop masculine traits. This better prepares him for life. This subject is one of increasing concern, but my basic concern in this study is with the role of women. There is an increasing desire among many women to make less distinctions between women and men. The ideals of femininity are fast disappearing.

When Christianity had a greater impact on the values of society, womanhood was held in high esteem. I can remember when ladies were held in high esteem. No man would have thought of keeping his seat while a lady was left standing. Men who smoked would either not smoke in the presence of a lady, or they would seek her permission. If a man used profanity or foul language in the hearing of a lady, he was quickly reminded by other men that such behavior would not be tolerated.

The lofty view of womanhood has suffered drastically. With this, the ideals of femininity have suffered loss. It is only when ladies see the lofty view of womanhood that they will seek to preserve the ideals of femininity.

A woman occupies a higher place of honor than that of a man. Men may rise to positions of honor, but a woman is born to a position of honor. It is hers simply because she is a woman. She does not need to earn it. She needs only to maintain it and enhance it.

The position of honor is seen in the honors that gentlemen bestow upon ladies. They open the door for them. They assist them when they put their coats on. Gentlemen rise and give ladies their seats when there is not room for all to be seated. They protect them in time of danger.

Women have made a tremendous contribution to society. This would be a drab world were it not for the feminine influence. Refinement and beauty are largely from the influence of women. Men would settle for barns as houses and nail kegs for chairs were it not for the uplifting influence of women.

I blame men, for the most part, for the disappearing of the high view of womanhood. Most of the remarks that are made about wives being in subjection

168

to their husbands is made in a jesting, noncomplimentary manner. It is the woman's place to enhance the esteem of womanhood, but it is the man's place to proclaim the esteem of womanhood. Most young ladies have never heard an elaboration on the exalted view of womanhood.

It is only when a lady sees the exalted view of womanhood that she will appreciate and aspire to the ideals of femininity. The ideals of femininity make demands. They are upheld by a price, but the reward is greater than the price.

It is frequently said, "I do not believe in a double standard for men and women." Yet, people who care still maintain somewhat of a double standard. Personally, I do believe in a double standard, not in the sense of a double moral standard, but in a double standard of protection. Because of her higher position of honor, a lady has more to lose than a man. That being true, she must take extra precautions, and we must take extra precautions for her.

I have a double standard for dress clothes and work clothes. If I have car trouble with a suit on, I am extra careful lest I get grease and dirt on my suit. If I have on work clothes, I do not see the same need for being careful though I may not want grease on them either. Ladies are the dress clothes. Men are the work clothes.

When a lady sees the exalted view of womanhood, she will recognize the value of the ideals of femininity. She will know what femininity is. She will be willing to take some steps to preserve and enhance the ideals of femininity. She has a high view of herself. She will not cheapen herself with all the fads and fashions introduced by those who know nothing of the value of womanhood.

The lady who sees the value of the ideals of femininity will seek to develop polish, poise, dignity, good manners, charm, and good taste. She will be interested in self-improvement. A woman with these interests would not dare stoop to competing for the attention of men by immodest dress. She is not only interested in modesty, but femininity. The question, "Should I wear slacks, and if so when?" is a question she takes seriously. The standards she sets for herself are based on the Scriptures and her own sense of God-given self-value, not on what everybody is doing. Blessed is the young man who finds such a young woman for a wife.

B. BASIC PERSONAL RELATIONSHIPS

Our Relationship with Our Neighbor. Jesus said, "Thou shalt love thy neighbour as thyself. On these two commandments [the other dealing with our love for God] hang all the law and the prophets" (Matthew 22:39-40). Paul said, "Thou shalt not commit adultery, Thou shalt not kill, Thou shalt not steal, Thou shalt not bear false witness, Thou shalt not covet; and if there be any other commandment, it is briefly comprehended in this saying, namely, Thou shalt love thy neighbour as

170

thyself. Love worketh no ill to his neighbour; therefore love is the fulfilling of the law" (Romans 13:9, 10).

Our life should be regulated by concern for others. Love for others demands of us that we live by the highest moral standards in our relationship with other people. Love considers violations of moral standards in our relationship to others as "working ill" to them. Love has the highest concern for the moral welfare of our neighbor. To fail to have this concern is to fail to love our neighbor. John supports this truth when he says, "By this we know that we love the children of God, when we love God, and keep his commandments" (1 John 5:2).

Love is concerned about the spiritual welfare of others. It was love that caused Paul to say, "I have great heaviness and continual sorrow in my heart. For I could wish that myself were accursed from Christ for my brethren, my kinsmen according to the flesh" (Romans 9:2, 3). He further says, "Brethren, my heart's desire and prayer to God for Israel is, that they might be saved" (Romans 10:1). Love motivates us to share the gospel with sinners.

It was on the basis of the concern of love for the spiritual welfare of others that Paul said, "For, brethren, ye have been called unto liberty; only use not liberty for an occasion to the flesh, but by love serve one another. For all the law is fulfilled in one word, even in this; Thou shalt love thy neighbour as thyself" (Galatians 5:13, 14). Liberty is not Christian liberty if it is not guided by love for others. Love never rides

171

roughshod over the feelings and concern of others in order to exercise its own rights. It gladly refrains from that which would hinder its spiritual influence upon others. As Paul said, "But if thy brother is grieved with thy meat, now walkest thou not charitably" (Romans 14:15).

Love is concerned about the physical needs of others. Jesus had compassion on the sick and on the hungry. Paul tells us, "As we have therefore opportunity, let us do good unto all men" (Galatians 6:10). Love accepts the guidance of wisdom as it exercises this concern, but it never forgets this concern.

Love is more than action. It is affectionate concern. Love for the poor is more than action. It is more than a welfare program. Paul evaluates action toward the poor that is not accompanied by affectionate concern. He says, "And though I bestow all my goods to feed the poor, and though I give my body to be burned, and have not charity, it profiteth me nothing" (1 Corinthians 13:3).

Love recognizes a fellow human being as one who is made in the image of God. The heart of every human being craves acceptance. Merely supplying food, shelter, and clothing will not meet this need. Within the framework of holiness and wisdom, love seeks to accept and be accepted. It extends the warm hand of friendship. It condescends "to men of low estate" (Romans 12:16). It is genuinely concerned about the total welfare of the individual. It is concerned about him as a human being.

Our Relationship with Other Christians. Jesus said, "By this shall all men know that ye are my disciples, if ye have love one to another" (John 13:35). We are to love all men, but we are to have a special love for fellow Christians. Paul said, "As we have therefore opportunity, let us do good unto all men, especially unto them who are of the household of faith" (Galatians 6:10).

Love for fellow Christians is not optional. It is a necessary fruit of the salvation experience. John makes this unquestionably clear in 1 John. To be a Christian is to walk in light. Those who are not Christians walk in darkness. John approaches the subject from every conceivable angle to make it clear that no one can be a Christian who does not love a fellow Christian.

In 1 John 2:9 he says, "He that saith he is in the light, and hateth his brother, is in darkness even until now." For one to say he is in the light is to profess that he is a Christian. John tells us that if a person says he is a Christian and hates his brother, he is walking in darkness. He further elaborates this point in 2:11. On the positive side he says, "He that loveth his brother abideth in light" (1 John 2:10).

John is very clear in his statements in chapter two, but lest he be misunderstood on the all-important issue he repeats his point and gives further elaboration in chapter three. In 3:10 he says, "Whosoever doeth not righteousness is not of God, neither he that loveth not his brother." In 3:14 he restates both the positive and the negative side, "We know that we have passed from death unto life, because we love the brethren. He that

173

loveth not his brother abideth in death."

In 3:15 he is very emphatic when he says, "Whosoever hateth his brother is a murderer: and ye know that no murderer hath eternal life abiding in him." It could not be made clearer that John means to say that it is impossible to hate a Christian and at the same time be a Christian. He is not just saying that to do so would be inconsistent.

Lest he be misunderstood, John makes clear the kind of love he is talking about. It is an attitude that results in action at the appropriate time. It is not just a matter of words. He explains: "But whoso hath this world's good, and seeth his brother have need, and shutteth up his bowels of compassion from him, how dwelleth the love of God in him? My little children, let us not love in word, neither in tongue; but in deed and in truth" (1 John 3:17, 18).

In chapter four John restates his insistence that only those who love their Christian brother can lay any rightful claim to salvation (1 John 4:7, 8, 20). God's love for us is to be the motivation of our love for others (1 John 4:9-11).

The Christian may have to deal with wrong attitudes in his heart toward fellow Christians, but he *does* deal with them. There is something in his heart that makes it impossible for his heart to become a seed-bed of hatred toward other Christians. He may not have the strongest love, but he has a love that can be cultivated.

Our Relationship with Our Enemies. Jesus said,

174

"Love your enemies, bless them that curse you, do good to them that hate you, and pray for them which despitefully use you, and persecute you" (Matthew 5:44). It was in the context of His teaching on loving our enemies that Jesus gave us the Golden Rule, "And as ye would that men should do to you, do ye also to them likewise" (Luke 6:31).

Paul tells us, "If it be possible, as much as lieth in you, live peaceably with all men." He goes further and warns us, "Dearly beloved, avenge not yourselves, but rather give place unto wrath: for it is written, Vengeance is mine; I will repay, saith the Lord." He concludes by saying, "Therefore if thine enemy hunger, feed him; if he thirst, give him drink: for in so doing thou shalt heap coals of fire on his head. Be not overcome of evil, but overcome evil with good" (Romans 12:18-21).

The Bible removes all possible grounds for hatred of people when it enjoins us to love our enemies. We are to seek ways of building bridges of communication with them. We are to act better toward them than they do toward us. We must respect them as human beings.

Biblical Admonitions with Regard to Our One-Another Relationships. Jesus tells us to "have peace one with another" (Mark 9:50). Through the symbolism of feet-washing He teaches that we are to be servants one of another (John 13:14).

Paul tells us that in honor we should prefer one another (Romans 12:10). We are to be of the same mind one to another (Romans 12:16). Paul admonishes us,

175

"Let us not therefore judge one another" (Romans 14:13). We are to edify one another (Romans 14:19). We are to admonish one another (Romans 15:14). In Galatians 6:2 Paul tells us, "Bear ye one another's burdens." We are admonished to be kind and tenderhearted one to another (Ephesians 4:32). We are to be forbearing and forgiving one to another (Ephesians 4:2, 32; Colossians 3:13). It is our responsibility to put away bitterness, evil speaking, and malice (Ephesians 4:31; James 4:11; 5:9; 1 Peter 4:9). We are to lie not one to another (Colossians 3:9). We are to put away envy and jealousy (Galatians 5:20, 21) and rejoice with them that rejoice and weep with them that weep (Romans 12:15).

12 | The Christian and the Material World

Introduction
A. The Positive Value of Material Things
   1. Man Is Told to Exercise Dominion over the Material Earth
   2. Material Possessions Are Referred to as a Blessing from God
   3. Poverty Is Considered as Being Undesirable
   4. We Are to Appreciate the Finer Things of Life
   5. Diligence Is To Be Rewarded with Material Gain
B. The Need for Observing One's Total Responsibility to God While Pursuing Material Gain
   1. The Right Means Must Be Followed
   2. The Poor Must Not Be Oppressed
   3. Priority Must Be Given to Seeking God and His Righteousness
C. Responsibilities To Be Faced by Those Who Possess Riches
   1. They Must Be Prepared to Overcome Temptations
   2. They Must Esteem Righteousness as Better than Riches

3. They Should Share Their Wealth with Those in Need

D. Responsibility to Support the Cause of Christ
   1. Supporting the Cause of Christ Is a Moral Obligation
   2. Our Giving Should Follow Scriptural Guidelines

INTRODUCTION

There has always been a tendency to look on material things as having negative value. The gnostics denied the human nature of Christ because they thought matter was evil. If He were good, they concluded that He could not have had a material body.

Asceticism with its disdain for enjoying material things has always sought to plague the conscientious mind. There is a contradiction between much of what we hear and much of what we see. We hear a person refer to material things as if he thinks we should have no concern for them, yet his own experience tells a different story. He has the best home, best furniture, best car, eats the best food, and wears the best clothes he can afford. Many sincere people feel guilty about having things of high quality.

The people who are caught in the contradiction stated above do not intend to be hypocritical when they proclaim one thing and experience another. On the one hand they feel obligated to depreciate material things.

On the other hand, they see the value of having material things. They can see some truth on both sides, but they cannot harmonize the truth. They operate with a false sense of guilt. They confuse both themselves and others.

A. THE POSITIVE VALUE OF MATERIAL THINGS

Man Is Told to Exercise Dominion over the Material Earth. Before man was created, it was decided that he should exercise dominion over the earth (Genesis 1:26). He was to use the animals, plants, and the earth itself to serve his needs. The physical body is dependent upon the earth for survival. It would seem very strange for God to make a man who was dependent upon the earth for his survival and was charged by God to exercise dominion over the material earth, if matter were at best a necessary evil. God has clearly placed a positive value on the material earth.

When God said that man was to have dominion over the earth, He meant for him to be a good steward of natural resources. He did not mean for him to have the least possible contact with the material world as if he were trying to avoid evil. Man is to be a good steward in exercising dominion over the earth. It is made for him to enjoy. The words of the psalmist give the proper value of the material earth when he says: "O LORD, how manifold are thy works! in wisdom hast thou made them all: the earth is full of thy riches" (Psalm 104:24).

Material Possessions Are Referred to as a Blessing

from God. In 1 Chronicles 29:12 David said in his prayer, "Both riches and honour come from thee." In response to Solomon's prayer for wisdom, God said, "Because this was in thine heart, and thou has not asked riches, wealth, or honour, nor the life of thine enemies, neither yet hast asked long life; but hast asked wisdom and knowledge for thyself, that thou mayest judge my people, over whom I have made thee king: Wisdom and knowledge is granted unto thee; and I will give thee riches, and wealth, and honour, such as none of the kings have had that have been before thee, neither shall there any after thee have the like (2 Chronicles 1:11, 12).

While Solomon is commended for putting wisdom above material possessions, it is also true that God's bestowal of material riches upon Solomon was considered a blessing. This would not have occurred if material things had been a necessary evil.

Poverty Is Considered as Being Undesirable. Proverbs warns that certain things will lead to poverty. For those who will not pay the price to succeed in life, poverty is viewed as a curse. The love of sleep will lead to poverty (Proverbs 20:13; 24:33, 34). "The drunkard and the glutton shall come to poverty: and drowsiness shall clothe a man with rags" (Proverbs 23:21). "He that followeth after vain persons shall have poverty enough" (Proverbs 28:19).

Poverty has devastating results. The writer of Proverbs wished to be spared poverty, "Lest I be poor, and steal, and take the name of my God in vain"

(Proverbs 30:9). Poverty destroys self-respect. It brings depression and despair. It is to be avoided, if it is at all possible by legitimate means.

We Are to Appreciate the Finer Things of Life. Paul said, "I have learned, in whatsoever state I am, therewith to be content. I know both how to be abased and I know how to abound: every where and in all things I am instructed both to be full and to be hungry, both to abound and to suffer need" (Philippians 4:11, 12).

When Paul said he had learned to be content under such circumstances, he did not mean that such things were desirable. He meant that he had been able to take a realistic approach to life. He had been able to make the adjustments that would keep undesirable circumstances from destroying his happiness.

In Philippians 4:8 Paul says, "Finally, brethren, whatsoever things are true, whatsoever things are honest, whatsoever things are just, whatsoever things are pure, whatsoever things are lovely, whatsoever things are of good report; if there be any virtue, and if there be any praise, think on these things." This verse has an uplifting influence. It turns our attention to excellence and the finer things of life. Poverty works against the direction of this verse.

In Revelation 21:10-21 John describes the New Jerusalem. It is made of gold, pearls, and precious stones. It would seem very strange for God to make the New Jerusalem appeal to us because it is made of gold, pearls, and precious stones, and at the same time make it wrong for us to have an interest in such things while in this life.

Diligence Is To Be Rewarded with Material Gain. "The hand of the diligent maketh rich" (Proverbs 10:4). "The thoughts of the diligent tend only to plenteousness" (Proverbs 21:5). "Seest thou a man diligent in his business? he shall stand before kings; he shall not stand before mean men" (Proverbs 22:29). "He that tilleth his land shall have plenty of bread" (Proverbs 28:19). The challenge of these verses encourages one to seek to improve his lot in life. We must abide by the Christian system of values and priorities, but within that context the Christian should seek to climb the ladder of success.

B. THE NEED FOR OBSERVING ONE'S TOTAL RESPONSIBILITY TO GOD WHILE PURSUING MATERIAL GAIN

The Right Means Must Be Followed. Jeremiah cries out against getting riches by unrighteous means. He says, "As the partridge sitteth on eggs, and hatcheth them not; so he that getteth riches, and not by right, shall leave them in the midst of his days, and at his end shall be a fool" (Jeremiah 17:11).

The means of making money must be submitted to the Christian value system. The laborer must not loaf on the job. The seller must tell the truth about his product. The repairman must not sell a person unneeded parts by taking advantage of his lack of knowledge. Women are frequently victims of this type of unethical practice.

The Poor Must Not Be Oppressed. Proverbs 22:16 reads: "He that oppresseth the poor to increase riches, and he that giveth to the rich, shall surely come to want." Isaiah warns: "Woe unto them that decree unrighteous decrees . . . to turn aside the needy from judgment, and to take away the right from the poor of my people, that widows may be their prey, and that they may rob the fatherless!" (Isaiah 10:1, 2).

The making of money must be guided by a concern for other people. This includes being careful not to oppress the poor, but it goes beyond that. It involves concern for others in the prices charged for our products and our services. Greed cannot be excused in prices charged by saying everybody else is doing it.

The principle of oppressing the poor goes beyond giving low wages and charging high prices. It involves keeping a good man down. We should be interested in seeing every man advance if he shows promise and works diligently. We should encourage him to develop his possibilities. We should not try to hang on to a good worker if we cannot offer him the possibility of developing his potential. Some employers rejoice when those who are faithful live to become their partner or even surpass them.

Priority Must Be Given to Seeking God and His Righteousness. Jesus said, "But seek ye first the kingdom of God, and his righteousness; and all these things shall be added unto you" (Matthew 6:33). This verse places a needed limitation on the pursuit of

183

material goods.

A Christian's plans must be submitted to the discipline of the Christian system of values, but they must also be submitted to further limitation. They must be submitted to: (1) The limitation called for by one's responsibility to Christian causes. (2) The limitation placed in many instances by the will of God. (3) The limitation placed by concern for others.

The first limitation tells us that we should not be so obligated to our secular job that we cannot be a good member of our church. A person should not spend so many hours on the job or in his office that he cannot be active in church and can attend only a minimum number of services. Neither should he be so dragged out by his work that he cannot be alert. He should have more than a tired body to offer to his church. The church needs to be reasonable in its demands, but the Christian needs to have something to offer. The interest in making money must not conflict with Matthew 6:33.

In many cases the will of God may make a complete change in a person's occupational plans. It is noble for a person to plan a successful career in life. However, we must never get so attached to these plans that we cannot submit them to the will of God. This is exactly what happens in many young lives when the call of God comes to do pastoral work, missionary work, or some other full-time work. If we have such a call of God, we should set aside our occupational plans and obey the call of God. In many cases this will involve a drastic cut in financial gain. Yet, the call of God must take priority.

When we seek the kingdom of God and His righteousness, we are guided by concern for others. We must not allow ourselves to get so busy that we have no time to show concern for others. This is particularly true with regard to our own families. They need *us*, not just what we can provide for them.

The rearing of a family is a divine responsibility. The needs of the family are high on the priority list. It is particularly important for those in full-time Christian service to keep this in mind. We cannot work on the assumption that if we will give ourselves to the service of God to the neglect of our family that God will see to it that our children develop as they should. Tragic results have proved otherwise. We cannot avoid the practical responsibilities in rearing children without suffering the consequences.

In the context of proper recognition of Christian values and putting the kingdom of God and His righteousness first, it is noble for a Christian to try to better himself financially. Christian young people should aspire to positions, careers, professions, business opportunities, etc., that represent a good stewardship of their natural talents. They should actually consider this as a divine responsibility in the light of man's responsibility to exercise dominion over the earth and the emphasis the Scriptures give to diligence, excellence, etc.

The Christian recognizes the distinctions that are generally referred to as secular and sacred, but he recognizes God as the God of the whole universe. His church life, home life, job, and leisure time are all viewed with the recognition that God is lord of all. He is the giver of every good and perfect gift (James 1:17). He sees the greatness of God in the created order. He recognizes the greatness of God who could create a universe and then create a man who could in the course of time unlock so many of the secrets of the universe. He recognizes the greatness of God when he sees the advancements of modern science. He thanks God for the material things he is able to enjoy. When the enjoyment of material things and modern conveniences does not lead to praise to God and a recognition of the greatness of God, the Christian view of material things has not been fully comprehended.

C. RESPONSIBILITIES TO BE FACED BY THOSE WHO POSSESS RICHES

They Must Be Prepared to Overcome Temptations. Paul warns: "But they that will be rich fall into temptation and a snare, and into many foolish and hurtful lusts, which drown men in destruction and perdition. For the love of money is the root of all evil: which while some coveted after, they have erred from the faith, and pierced themselves through with many sorrows" (1 Timothy 6:9, 10).

There are certain temptations that are connected with the possession and pursuit of riches. There is a sense of security that goes with possessions. This causes those who have possessions to run the risk of trusting in riches. Paul tells Timothy to "charge them that are rich in this world, that they be not highminded, nor trust in uncertain riches, but in the living God, who giveth us richly all things to enjoy" (1 Timothy 6:17).

The pressures of the business world are a real test of character. The pressure from competition, the persuasion of a friend or partner whose principles are not so high as one's own, and the feeling everybody is doing it must be resisted. There is always the problem: "Well, maybe this one time will not matter." There is the problem of that which is legally acceptable, but may not be morally acceptable. There is the pressure of paying off a loan. Only those strongest in character can withstand.

Those who are in the higher income brackets are frequently invited to social events that do not abide by Christian standards. There is the pressure to go because it is good for the business to know people socially. There is the pressure to go lest one be offensive, or be considered a misfit. Once the person is at the social event there is the pressure to participate in that which is either wrong or questionable.

Jesus said, "A rich man shall hardly enter into the kingdom of heaven. . . . It is easier for a camel to go through the eye of a needle, than for a rich man to enter into the kingdom of God" (Matthew 19:23, 24). There are many reasons for this. Perhaps the greatest reason is the truth spoken by Jesus, "For where your treasure is, there will your heart be also" (Matthew 6:21). The rich man's interest is diverted away from God by his possessions. He does not think he has time for God. His dependence upon riches makes it hard for him to feel the need of God. Repentance may require changes in business habits or life styles that he is not ready to make. His friendship with sinners may have a hold upon him that keeps him from coming to Christ.

The Biblical warnings to those who are rich, no doubt, account for much of the play-down that is given to material possessions. Yet, we must not make up our minds about material possessions without also considering the hazards of poverty. As has already been pointed out earlier in the chapter, poverty is considered undesirable in the Scriptures. Poverty is depressing. It kills initiative. It destroys self-respect. It places a severe limitation on the realization of Christian ideals. There is very little room for excellence. Bitterness and resentment frequently occur. While riches presents its problems and temptations, so does proverty.

The Book of Proverbs sums up the matter well when it says: "Give me neither poverty nor riches; feed me with food convenient for me: lest I be full, and deny thee, and say, Who is the LORD? or lest I be poor, and steal, and take the name of my God in vain" (Proverbs 30:8, 9).

There are a few people who can be wealthy and maintain a Christian testimony. The majority of people are better off if they are somewhere between poverty and wealth. In this way, they are less likely to fall into certain temptations than they would be if they were extremely poor or extremely wealthy.

They Must Esteem Righteousness as Better than Riches. The psalmist tells us: "A little that a righteous man hath is better than the riches of many wicked" (Psalm 37:16). Proverbs 16:8 reads: "Better is a little with righteousness than great revenues without right." According to Proverbs 19:1: "Better is the poor that walketh in his integrity, than he that is perverse in his lips, and is a fool."

Righteousness must be viewed as an asset in life, not a handicap. Righteousness comes at a price, but so does everything else that is valuable. The person who views righteousness as a handicap imposed upon him by his religion will consider it a burden to be borne, not a blessing to be shared. He will bemoan the fact that he cannot do like his unscrupulous competitors. He will run a high risk of being crushed by the load and falling into sin.

It is only when righteousness is viewed as better than riches that a person can make an accurate assessment of his assets. No amount of riches can make up for lack of righteousness. The rich person who lacks righteousness is poor. The poor man who has righteousness is rich.

They Should Share Their Wealth with Those in Need. Paul said to Timothy: "Charge them that are rich in this world . . . that they do good, that they be rich in good works, ready to distribute, willing to communicate; laying up in store for themselves a good

189

foundation against the time to come, that they may lay hold on eternal life" (1 Timothy 6:17-19). The words that are translated, "ready to distribute, willing to communicate" mean: "liberal, generous, ready to share." Such action on the part of the rich is laying up treasures for the life to come.

It is well and good for us to be concerned that help given to the underprivileged actually helps. We need to be concerned that what is given to relieve a need is used to relieve that need instead of being used to buy alcohol. There is a place for abiding by Paul's admonition to the Thessalonians when he said: "For even when we were with you, this we commanded you, that if any would not work, neither should he eat" (2 Thessalonians 3:10).

At the same time there are needs for precaution. The Christian must have a heart, and must find ways to show his concern. Wisdom must find valid means to help. The Christian must be more than an expert on when not to help. Those who are blessed with wealth must do more than just help when approached. They must seek means of sharing their wealth to help relieve misery and suffering.

It is interesting to note that apart from Paul's mention of thanks to those who had helped him, the only mention in the early church of an offering is in connection with helping saints who had material need (Acts 11:27-30; 1 Corinthians 16:1, 2; 2 Corinthians 8:1—9:15; Romans 15:25-27). Paul mentioned some guidelines to Timothy to follow in helping aged widows

190

(1 Timothy 5:1-16).

D. RESPONSIBILITY TO SUPPORT
THE CAUSE OF CHRIST

Supporting the Cause of Christ Is a Moral Obligation. Concerning the offering from Macedonia and Achaia for the poor saints at Jerusalem Paul says: "It hath pleased them verily; and their debtors they are. For if the Gentiles have been made partakers of their spiritual things, their duty is also to minister unto them in carnal things" (Romans 15:27). By carnal things, Paul meant material things. This principle is further elaborated in Galatians 6:6: "Let him that is taught in the word communicate unto him that teacheth in all good things." The word "communicate" as it is used here means share. The idea is that the one taught spiritual truth should share his material goods with his teacher. It is this obligation that caused Paul to say: "Even so hath the Lord ordained that they which preach the gospel should live by the gospel" (1 Corinthians 9:14).

There is the cost of supporting the pastor and others who give their time required for making a living to Christian causes. There is the cost of building and maintaining the church building. Those who identify with a local church are morally obligated to share in paying the bills of the church.

Our Giving Should Follow Scriptural Guidelines. The Christian should first give himself to God (2

Corinthians 8:5). He should give with a willing mind (2 Corinthians 8:11, 12). He should give liberally (2 Corinthians 8:2). He should give according to what he has (2 Corinthians 8:12). He should give "not grudgingly, or of necessity: for God loveth a cheerful giver" (2 Corinthians 9:7).

While there is a basic moral obligation in supporting the church, there is also a place for love that goes beyond moral obligation. Paul's statement to Timothy, "Let the elders that rule well be counted worthy of double honour," calls for a show of love in supporting the elder (pastor), not simply living up to a moral obligation. Support for the various causes that promote the cause of Christ calls for giving that is motivated by love.

Many Christians have chosen tithing as a basic means of support for the cause of Christ. Not all are agreed on their reasons for tithing. Some take the position that the Old Testament Law is still in effect. Others tithe because they feel we should at least do as well in our giving as was required of the Old Testament saints.

13 | The Christian's Use of Leisure Time

Introduction
A. The Light and Serious in Proper Perspective
  1. There Is a Place for Leisure
  2. The Serious Side of Life Surpasses the Light Side in Value
B. Guidelines in the Use of Leisure Time
  1. There Are Positive Considerations
  2. There Is a Negative Side
C. Areas of Concern
  1. What about Theater Attendance?
  2. What about Television?
  3. What about Dancing and Petting?
  4. What about Church Sponsored Events?
  5. What about Sunday?
D. Concluding Observations

INTRODUCTION

By leisure time is meant that time that is not taken

193

up in one's employment, responsibilities in the home, and church responsibilities. This is the part of a person's time in which he engages in pleasure, a hobby, etc.

What to do in our leisure time places a real test on our ability to live up to the Christian system of values. In what pleasures can we engage? From what must we refrain?

A person's ability to use his leisure time is a test of his ingenuity. Will leisure time result in boredom because of nothing to do? Or, will it be a time of joy and satisfaction?

A. THE LIGHT AND SERIOUS IN PROPER PERSPECTIVE

There Is a Place for Leisure. The conscientious mind is sometimes ensnared by the idea that in a world of so much sin and sorrow there is no place for a lighter side of life. All possible energies must be spent in witnessing and other moral and spiritual pursuits. It is felt that it is wrong to take a vacation.

In view of the horrible destiny of those who reject Christ and the ruinous effects of sin in their lives, it is easy to see how one can fall prey to the logic above. It is good for us that we have an incident in the life of Jesus and the apostles that gives Jesus' view on the validity of having leisure time.

Jesus had sent the apostles out two by two on a preaching and healing ministry (Mark 6:7-13). The

194

apostles returned to Jesus and gave Him a report on what they had done. "And he said unto them, Come ye yourselves apart into a desert place, and rest a while: for there were many coming and going, and they had no leisure so much as to eat" (Mark 6:30, 31).

It is evident that in the throngs of people who were moving about there were people who had spiritual needs. Yet, Jesus and His apostles sought to go away and rest for a while. Jesus did not work on the assumption that He and the apostles could not rest until everyone's spiritual needs were met. It is true that the people followed them and interfered with their rest (Mark 6:32-44). At the same time, Jesus' words in Mark 6:31 approve the position that leisure time for rest is valid.

The Serious Side of Life Surpasses the Light Side in Value. Which makes the greatest contribution to happiness, the light or the serious? We are not to assume that the light is always wrong and the serious is always right. However, it is important in a study of ethics to see the relative value of the light and serious to happiness.

By the light, we mean thrills, excitement, and entertainment. If a person sees the light side of life as the chief ingredient of a happy life, he will run into two problems: (1) Sin will be enticing because it offers more quick thrills than righteousness. (2) The lighter experiences will tend to keep him from fulfilling the demanding obligations of life.

For the person who is willing to follow it, sin stands ready to offer a quick thrill. A person may be

195

caused to forget his problems by alcohol. He may enter a state of ecstasy by a trip on drugs. Sexual immorality offers momentary pleasure. There are occasional thrills in the pathway of righteousness. Not all entertainment and excitement are wrong. But the pathway of right-eousness does not always offer an immediate thrill.

The person who thinks thrills, excitement, and entertainment are the chief ingredients of life finds work, study, and various means of self-improvement boring. He is constantly looking for an escape from the responsibilities on the serious side of life. He gives it the least he can. Yet, righteousness prescribes many responsibilities that are on the serious side of life.

If a person expects to find most of his happiness in the lighter experiences, he will not be able to take an honest look at sin and righteousness in matters of recreation and entertainment. He feels that to deny himself experiences that are popular among others is to deny himself happiness. He will look hard for reasons to call what he wants to do right. He will be blind to things that will indicate that what he wants to do is wrong.

Paul puts the light and the serious in proper perspective when he said to Timothy: "For bodily exercise profiteth little: but godliness is profitable unto all things, having promise of the life that now is, and of that which is to come" (1 Timothy 4:8).

Bodily exercise would be in the area of sports and recreation. Thus, it represents the lighter side of life. It has some value. This is not to be overlooked, but it is surpassed in value by godliness. Godliness has value both in this life and in the next.

Godliness refers to reverential living. It is a life that is lived in submission to God. Godliness is clearly on the serious side of life. It is demanding, but it is also rewarding. In 1 Timothy 4:10 Paul says, "For therefore we both labour and suffer reproach, because we trust in the living God." To labor and suffer is to pay a price. Yet Paul was willing to pay the price since godliness has the promise both of this life and the next. The "therefore" of verse 10 connects this verse with the promise of verse 8.

Godliness has the promise of the life that now is. This means that it forms the basis of happiness in this life. It is demanding. Yet it is the basis for happiness. Our relationship with God gives us forgiveness of sins. Since God forgives us, we can forgive ourselves. Godliness involves righteous living and dedication to worthy objectives in life. These form the basis of self-respect and self-esteem.

Self-respect and self-esteem form the foundation of happiness. There can be no happiness apart from a good self-image. There can be no self-respect and self-esteem apart from the experience of forgiveness, moral uprightness, and dedication to worthwhile goals. These come from the serious side of life, not from the light side.

The light side of life has its contribution to make. _ It gives needed rest and relaxation of the body, the mind, and the nervous system. When subjected to the sanctifying influence of Christian values, it offers legitimate thrills. The lighter experiences of life are like a dessert after a meal. Like dessert the lighter side is not good for our whole diet.

The person whose life does not have the ingredients of forgiveness of sin, moral uprightness, and dedication to worthy causes as a foundation has an empty life. It is a life of boredom, depression, despair, and misery. The victim of such a life is a prime target for alcohol, drugs, immorality, and unrighteous entertainment. He has no foundation for happiness. He can only hope to be delivered out of his misery by escape from reality.

The person who has the ingredients of forgiveness of sin, moral uprightness, and dedication to worthy causes has the foundation for a happy life. He finds the lighter moments of life refreshing, helpful, and enjoyable. He has to deal with problems in life, but he does not need to resort to alcohol, drugs, and immorality. He can face reality. He does not have to escape from it. Such a person is not so dependent upon thrills, entertainment, and excitement that he cannot recognize that which is sin and depart from it. His life is too full to find it necessary to justify the questionable.

B. GUIDELINES IN THE USE OF LEISURE TIME

There Are Positive Considerations. A holy life is more than the subtraction of sin or the elimination of evil. We do not just take that which society provides and label it as right or wrong. We do not have to reject everything that society provides, but neither are we to simply place our labels "right" and "wrong" on what they provide. We must be creative in our own minds.

We are to search for the good in life so we can experience it, not just search for evil so we can avoid it. Paul admonishes us to "cleave to that which is good" (Romans 12:9). In Philippians 4:8 he exhorts us, "If there be any virtue, and if there be any praise, think on these things." This is the positive side of holy living.

While the lighter side has its legitimate place in the use of leisure time, there are many things of more substance that can occupy our time. Such things as reading and hobbies fit into this category. A creative mind and a little will power should be able to deal a death blow to boredom.

There Is a Negative Side. Since we live in a world where sin has touched so many things, we cannot avoid being negative. We must critically examine things. No part of human experiences has been more subjected to the influences of sin than the area of pleasure and entertainment.

There are special reasons for being concerned about sin in the area of pleasure and entertainment. There has been no other area of life where there has been so much justification of sin. By argument and intimidation defenses are made for sin. Everybody is doing it. Times have changed. It is a person's own business what he does in private. A person is young only once. Everybody sows his wild oats. There is nothing else to do. So and so does it, and he is a good Christian. These and many other arguments are used to coax the unprepared person, especially the young, into sin.

Another reason for being concerned is that when sin works its way into pleasure and entertainment it appeals to bodily appetites and lusts. The mood is light. The will-power is weak. Yet, the consequences can be serious. A young girl may lose her purity. A young man may become a victim of alcohol. A young girl may become addicted to drugs. There is loss of self-respect. There are lifetime regrets. For many, it is the road of no return. The lighter side of life can have serious consequences.

It is imperative that we have a deep conviction that righteousness is good and sin is bad. Nothing short of this conviction will enable us to willingly and confidently call sin *sin* in the area of pleasure and entertainment. This conviction prepares one to "hunger and thirst after righteousness" (Matthew 5:6) and to "abhor that which is evil" (Romans 12:9). Without this attitude there will be spiritual blindness. No amount of arguments can convince us of truth that would alter our experience. Twenty-twenty moral vision is impossible apart from hungering and thirsting after righteousness and abhoring evil.

Once the attitude is right about moral issues, the morality of the Ten Commandments goes beyond the letter of the law. Until the attitude is right, no amount of arguments will cause a person to see beyond the letter of the law. Our basic responsibility, therefore, is to sell people on the idea that righteousness is good and sin is bad.

The person whose heart is right believes that happiness is found with the discovery and experience of truth. He knows well the meaning of Jesus' words: "And ye shall know the truth, and the truth shall make you free" (John 8:32). He is not afraid to board the ship of honesty. He knows that it leads to truth and that truth is good for him. He does not have to engage in label-changing with reference to things he would like to do. He knows that if it is right and good that truth will uphold it. He knows that if it is sinful he will be better off if he quits. He considers it a blessing to know the truth.

The person with the attitude described above understands well the words of Jesus: "Ye have heard that it was said by them of old time, Thou shalt not commit adultery: but I say unto you, That whosoever looketh on a woman to lust after her hath committed adultery with her already in his heart" (Matthew 5: 27, 28).

The problem comes when a person wants to live on the outer edges of what is right. He is more interested in not giving up too much than he is in not giving up enough. The whole moral picture will be confusing to such a person. He will not be able to distinguish the arguments of those who are justifying sin from those who are defending righteousness. Such a person is clearly not sold on the fact that righteousness is good.

The person who is sold on the priceless value of purity may not know where the outer edges of right are,

201

but he knows where the safe zone is. As Proverbs 11:3 reads: "The integrity of the upright shall guide them." He may not feel that his action is absolutely necessary, but he knows it is safe. He may not be willing to dogmatically prescribe his path of action to others, but he feels comfortable in following it for himself.

The young person with the right attitude about purity can establish safe guidelines for courtship. The young lady who sees the value of purity and the high honor of womanhood will be able to dress modestly. The young man who values purity knows what to do about dirty jokes.

Christian ethics does not prepare an infallible list of do's and don'ts for every area of life. This would be legalism. In Christian ethics, there are areas where each person has a safe set of do's and don'ts that serve his own purposes. He shares them, but he does not feel that the other person must adopt them as a set of laws. He does expect to find common interests and mutual respect among those who are hungering and thirsting after righteousness.

First John 2:15, 16 offers basic principles to test pleasure and entertainment. It reads: "Love not the world, neither the things that are in the world. If any man love the world, the love of the Father is not in him. For all that is in the world, the lust of the flesh, and the lust of the eyes, and the pride of life, is not of the Father, but is of the world."

The word "world" is not synonymous with "earth" in this verse. It refers to a world system that operates on the principles of the lust of the flesh, the lust of the eyes, and the pride of life. The world promotes that which comes from man's base nature. It does not build on nor appeal to the high, the lofty, the noble, and the holy. It works on principles that are contrary to God. It is against God. To love it is to fail to love God.

People who are bored with life and are unhappy have a limited capacity to enjoy things. They can respond only to things that appeal to bodily appetites. Bodily appetites offer immediate pleasure, but the pleasure soon dies away. The process must be repeated. The boredom of life on the part of so many gives rise to the interjection of the cheap and the base into so much entertainment. Even people who should know better at times feel obligated to sneak something in that is off-color.

The Christian who has a proper appreciation for righteousness will neither participate in nor condone that which issues from and appeals to the base in life. Paul gives us a very helpful principle along this line in Romans 1:32. He says: "Who knowing the judgment of God, that they which commit such things are worthy of death, not only do the same, but have pleasure in them that do them." Paul is condemning the idea of having pleasure in the wrong done by others. If it is wrong to tell a dirty joke, it is wrong to delight in hearing someone else tell one.

Closely related to the principles involved in 1 John 2:15, 16 and Romans 1:32 is what is taught in Romans

12:9. Paul says, "Abhor that which is evil; cleave to that which is good." When we abhor the base and sinful and refuse to take delight in the sins of others, we will both develop sound convictions, and a disdain for that which is wrong.

C. AREAS OF CONCERN

There will be no attempt to be complete in listing areas of concern. The basic principles discussed in connection with the areas considered will be helpful also in areas not mentioned.

What about Theater Attendance? The principles discussed above in connection with 1 John 2:15, 16; Romans 1:32; and Romans 12:9 are helpful. The basic question for one to decide is this: What will a person's attitude be toward movies if he "abhors that which is evil, and cleaves to that which is good"? Will he enjoy going if he abhors the evil which he sees? Most of us do not enjoy abhorring evil well enough to invite opportunites that require this reaction on our part. It is quite obvious that a person who is hungering and thirsting after righteousness would not find many movies that would suit his taste.

Another problem arises with regard to whether to attend the few that would not be rejected by one who abhors evil and cleaves to the good. The things a person must decide in cases like this are: How can I be sure that it is morally respectable without running the risk of going to one that is not? Will my example in attending one that passes inspection be misunderstood? Will someone use my example as a reason for going to one that is not acceptable? What will it do to my testimony? What does my concern for the moral and spiritual welfare of others tell me to do? We may not be able to develop a dogmatic case for our position, but the person who takes these questions seriously and has the proper concern will be able to find a satisfactory position.

What about Television? Some people equate television and theater attendance so far as ethical involvements are concerned. Certainly, there is a common area of concern. Television programs that do not pass the test of 1 John 2:15, 16; Romans 1:32; and Romans 12:9 should be rejected. The rejection will be natural to those who abhor evil and cleave to that which is good. We do not have to reject every program where there is the slightest bit of evil. We do need to abhor the evil. When we abhor the evil, we will reject the program if we find ourselves having to abhor evil through very much of the program. We will continue to watch a program only as we enjoy it. If our enjoyment of the program requires us to enjoy sin, we sin by enjoying it.

There are two basic differences in watching television and attending the theater: (1) The question of testimony is not usually the same. (2) On television there is a greater selectivity. There are many wholesome programs as well as many that are not.

In addition to the moral concerns related to television, there is the concern for its drawing power to keep people, especially the young, from worthwhile pursuits. Televison, for many, has an irresistible drawing power that interferes with reading, study, sociability, development of hobbies, etc. Blessed is the person who can exercise proper control over his television set!

What about Dancing and Petting? The only person who is prepared to answer this question is the one who sees the true value of sexual purity. Such a person will heed the admonition of Paul when he said, "Flee fornication" (1 Corinthians 6:18).

Are dancing and petting consistent with fleeing fornication? Do dancing and petting arouse passions in the body that weaken a person's resistance to immorality? If a person loves purity, these questions are not hard to answer. If he does not, these questions mean very little to him.

When courtship exalts the pure, the holy, the lofty, and the beautiful, it forms the foundation for high respect and admiration for each other. Each feels that the other is worthy of protection. It is a time when two people get to know each other as persons. In such a courtship physical passions are held in check. The sacredness of sexual purity is protected.

What about Church Sponsored Events? A church sponsored event is not the occasion for one to exercise his Christian liberty to the fullest. What happens on these occasions receives semi-official church approval. There needs to be a high regard for the highest standards within the church on such occasions. Church sponsored events must not sink to the level of the lowest standards in the church.

What about Sunday? It is admitted that there are no authoritative statements in the Scriptures about what should and should not be done on Sunday. However, if we are going to consider it a holy day in any sense of the word, we need to be concerned that what we do does not violate that principle. I think we need to rethink our *attitude* about Sunday. Correct Sunday observance begins with an attitude of respect for the day.

D. CONCLUDING OBSERVATIONS

I trust that the following convictions have been developed as you have gone through this study: (1) Holiness is at the very heart and core of Christianity; it is not optional. (2) Righteousness is good. (3) A proper observance of Christian values is the foundation of a meaningful, happy life. (4) Only those who hunger and thirst after righteousness can develop a fully Christian view of ethics. (5) Those who do hunger and thirst after righteousness need not be bound by the feeling of incapability when it comes to the matter of rendering moral judgments. (6) The reward for ethical living far exceeds the price.

CPSIA information can be obtained at www.ICGtesting.com
Printed in the USA
LVOW040749111211

258834LV00001B/10/A